Butlin's
75 YEARS OF FUN!

SYLVIA ENDACOTT AND SHIRLEY LEWIS

The
History
Press

For Paul Winterforde-Young
Our Inspiration

First published 2011

The History Press
The Mill, Brimscombe Port
Stroud, Gloucestershire, GL5 2QG
www.thehistorypress.co.uk

British Library Cataloguing in Publication Data.
A catalogue record for this book is available from the British Library.

ISBN 978 0 7524 5863 2

Typesetting and origination by The History Press
Printed in Great Britain
Manufacturing managed by Jellyfish Print Solutions Ltd

Contents

Acknowledgements

This book has been made possible by the generosity of people who have loaned photographs, postcards, prints and sketches, allowing us to help the reader to understand Billy Butlin and his ideas for the enjoyment of his campers.

We have endeavoured to trace the ownership of all photographs but if we have inadvertently missed anyone, we apologise. Many of the images used are from the joint collection of Sylvia Endacott and Shirley Lewis. Extra special thanks are due to Ron Stanway.

The following individuals have agreed to their illustrations being included: Derek Aldridge, Beryl Allen, Roger Billington, Sylvia Gunner, Gerry Cable, Dizzy Cable, Andy King, Terry Shearing, Mike Smith, Kay Wise and we especially acknowledge use of the Butlin's Archives.

Research was additionally carried out by Pat Baxter, Anne Smith, and Diana Winterforde -Young.

Thanks also to the following for their help with proofreading, encouragement and support: Kevin Burge, Mil Chimley, Cathy Jupp, Roger Smith, Tricia Smith, and Sheila Stanway.

Also by the Authors

Reflections of Bognor Regis

Introduction

We both worked for the Butlin's company from 1958 to 1996, Sylvia as Personnel Manager (known as HR today) and Shirley responsible for the Nursery Service provision of the company. Latterly, as local historians, we have both been involved in talks, displays and internet information on the history of the company.

This publication will not cover every aspect of Butlin's long and detailed history, but we have endeavoured to show the diversity of the organisation from the beginning and the width of its operation.

Billy Butlin started with his fun fairs and holiday centres, but there has been much expansion over the years, not appreciated by everyone. Billy's original slogan 'Our True Intent Is All For Your Delight' was used across buildings and brochures for many years. It is remembered by guests whose first visit was as a teenager and who now return annually with their grandchildren.

In a 1961 programme a question was asked, 'What manner of man is this Billy Butlin?' The response was:

> He is publicity conscious and blasts his name in print with all gimmick guns firing because it is good for business. He is generous ... he is a sort of soft-centred hard caramel of a man. He is a personality in his own right, but shy in the presence of lesser people until he has won their confidence. In short, he is BILLY BUTLIN – loved by his campers, respected as 'The Gov'nor' by his staff.

This was true from the very beginning and remained throughout the time that he remained in charge.

We have primarily viewed Butlin's from the perspective of the customers, but include some staff memories. Entertainers with their red coats are synonymous with the company but there are many thousands of other employees, working in accommodation, catering, security, shops and bars, retail, amusement parks etc., all of whom provide a vital service to the guests but who are usually forgotten.

We have used the nursery department as a representative department as they had a specific place in the history of the company providing facilities for our special guests – children.

As we delved into the history of the company and read various publications, company brochures, programmes and staff magazines, we continually found extra facets to the company – another competition, or another association with charities or national organisations – and we have had to make some tough decisions about which information we had space to include and which had to be left out.

Since we both left the employment of the company there have been many changes, with a reduction in the number of centres, hotels and their ancillary services. However, the current organisation is specifically working to a future goal which Billy would have approved of. Chalets are being removed to be replaced by hotels, but this will not detract from the provision of a holiday service providing enjoyment for guests of all ages. Moving on is important, but the past should not be forgotten.

For ease of reading we have primarily referred to Sir William Butlin MBE as Billy, the name by which he was known to his staff and guests. We apologise if we have not included your memory, but hope that you enjoy these images and that they will prompt your own happy recollections.

Sylvia Endacott & Shirley Lewis, 2011

one

Billy Butlin

Much has been written about Billy over the years but only the basics will be touched upon here. He was born William Heygate Edmund Colbourne Butlin, on 29 September 1899 in Cape Town, South Africa, where his father William, a country gentleman, and his mother Bertha, a bakery worker, had emigrated some years earlier from Great Britain. On the break-up of his parents' marriage, Billy returned to England. He moved to Canada in about 1910 and it was here he received the majority of his education. Billy left school early and gained employment in Toronto with a wastepaper company before moving on to work for Eaton's, a large Toronto Departmental Store. After the outbreak of the First Wold War he joined the Canadian Army as a bugler and drummer boy, serving in France as a stretcher bearer. After the war he returned to Eaton's but eventually became restless and returned to England, arriving in Liverpool on 17 February 1921 with only £5 in his pocket, allegedly earned during the journey over.

He travelled to Bristol, joining his fairground family and friends who took him under their wing. It was here that he learnt many 'tricks of the trade' that remained with him throughout his career. In 1922 he employed his first member of staff, to whom he paid £1 per week and provided a white coat with the letter 'B' on the breast pocket. He painted his stall red and white and this was to be the birth of his image.

On a visit to the 'Cunningham Young Man's Holiday Camp' he noticed that everyone stayed in small lodges and on the last night everyone congregated to sing 'Auld Lang Syne'. He emulated these two features when his camps were born.

Billy was an entrepreneur and by 1925 had realised that travelling fairs were on the decline. He made the decision to set up on his own with permanent amusement parks based at seaside resorts. By 1932 he was operating nine parks, several of which had zoos attached.

An important aspect of his life story was his work during the Second World War. It is generally known that he was asked to allow his sites at Clacton and Skegness, and those currently under construction at Ayr, Filey and Pwllheli, to be used by the Armed Forces for training purposes prior to their embarkation.

However, he was also involved in the provision of facilities for troops and their families, and the establishment of clubs for the large number of women working in munitions factories, thus providing them with entertainment, a social life and subsequent friendships. These clubs, known as the '21 Clubs', also provided an opportunity for troops returning to Britain to relax from the tensions of war, and socialise with comrades.

His wartime work was aptly rewarded when he received the MBE in 1945 'for service during the war', and later a Knighthood for 'Services to the Church'. Neither of these awards comes readily to mind when talking about the entrepreneur who started the major UK holiday environment; the man whose name became synonymous with leisure and entertainment in the 1930s, much loved, and sometimes maligned, but definitely an integral part of British Social History.

At the age of fifteen, W.E. Butlin (hereafter called Billy) was a drummer boy in the Canadian army, and on arrival in England was stationed at the Sandgate Camp near Folkestone in Kent. He later moved to France as part of the reinforcement for the Canadian Mounted Rifles, becoming one of the youngest soldiers to serve in France during the First World War. Billy said that the horrors he had witnessed had been 'the making' of him. Later in life he became known as the 'Greatest Showman of Them All' but by his staff as simply the 'Guv'nor'. An ideas man, he rapidly became a 'legend in his time'.

Albeit on a small scale, Billy carried out the first ever survey of the English on holiday, observing social history from his hoopla stall when he witnessed despondent holidaymakers sheltering from the rain, unable to return to their guesthouses until evening. He came upon the idea to provide accommodation, catering and entertainment all under one roof and for a set price of no more than a week's wage. By the time he reached thirty-four he was earning £25,000 a year, had moved out of his caravan and bought his first house.

Billy introduced 'dodgems' into England from the US, with their first appearance being at Skegness Amusement Park, Whitsun 1928. A few months later he acquired the sole agency for the sale of these in Europe. In 1929, he expanded the dodgems franchise to the Mablethorpe Amusement Park.

Billy's mother, Bertha, with her two nieces in 1929, when she managed his Mablethorpe Park. Bertha insisted the staff wore collar and tie and Billy provided a white jacket with blue collar and cuffs. A blue 'B' was embroidered on the breast pocket. There were no side pockets as the canny Billy didn't 'want takings popped in them!'

For Billy, being involved with charity events held locally to a camp was always a priority. In towns across Britain today there are many clubs, halls and groups who owe their very existence to the generosity of Billy Butlin or the special fundraising events held on his camps.

Billy was regularly seen on camps during the holiday season, as here in 1937, and he liked nothing more than to mingle with holidaymakers, signing autographs as he went.

Here we see Billy with Gracie Fields enjoying a ride on one of his rollercoasters. He was often seen entertaining people from the show business world and Billy felt all publicity was good advertising, particularly from visiting celebrities who often had their own publicity aide who would liaise with the camp press officers.

Billy worked with people from all walks of life, one of whom was Lord Mountbatten. Billy was involved in a large amount of charity work and this brought him into contact with many members of the Royal Family.

Above Billy's Skegness camp was renamed HMS *Royal Arthur* in 1939, after an 1889 cruiser. This new land base was used throughout the war for training many thousands of Royal Navy seamen. By the end of 1946 more than 250,000 navy personnel had experienced a far more arduous time than any holidaymakers before or after hostilities. One of those seamen, David Jacobs, went on to become a top BBC radio presenter.

Left Training during the war took many forms but one of the most important for the sailors was the ability to be able to fix their hammocks. Here the men can be seen practising 'slinging their hammocks' outside their chalets ready for the day when they would join a ship. In 2003 a commemorative obelisk was erected to reflect the camp's involvement during the war and all the men stationed there.

Right Like all good service sites throughout the war, entertainment was paramount and here we see just one of the programmes for the newly-named holiday centre. Meanwhile, in 1943 and trying to spoil the entertainment, Lord Haw Haw, the Nazi Minister for Propaganda, in his daily broadcast on the radio, announced the sinking of HMS *Royal Arthur* by German U-Boats in the North Sea.

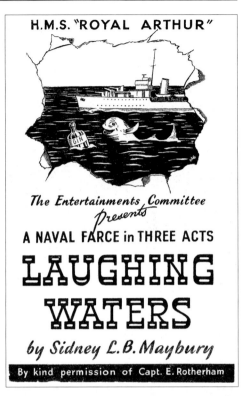

H.M.S. "ROYAL ARTHUR"

The Entertainments Committee Presents

A NAVAL FARCE in THREE ACTS

LAUGHING WATERS

by Sidney L.B. Maybury

By kind permission of Capt. E. Rotherham

Below Eventually used as the Boating Lake for holidaymakers, it is seen here being utilized by the Royal Navy for various training exercises. This area was originally excavated by Billy as part of his sea defences to prevent regular flooding in the area. Incidentally, it was to become the longest boating lake in the country, at 2,000 yards long and 50 yards wide.

Harry Warner, a close friend of Billy's, was responsible for transforming the newly constructed Filey site for war use and then became Commander of the newly formed Home Guard on the site. At one stage the former Lance Corporal Butlin even enlisted as a private in this Home Guard Group.

Here we can see Billy (third from the right) outside the Officers' Mess on the Clacton Camp. It was originally intended as a Prisoner of War camp, but, due to lack of prisoners at the time, it became a training centre for the Army Pioneer Corps with the tennis courts used as a parade ground and the swimming pool used for training commandos.

Right This photograph shows troops on the
parade ground at Clacton. One imagines that a
'Luxury Holiday Camp' was the last thing on
the minds of the men as they marched past this
corner. How many of these men returned to
Clacton after the war?

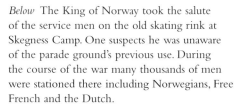

Below The King of Norway took the salute
of the service men on the old skating rink at
Skegness Camp. One suspects he was unaware
of the parade ground's previous use. During
the course of the war many thousands of men
were stationed there including Norwegians, Free
French and the Dutch.

Left Billy also became involved in opening '21 Clubs', named after the 21st Army Corps. Over 2,000 visited some of these clubs nightly, paying 2s 6d for tea, coffee and cakes. Very weak lager was also available, at 5d per glass. Billy was one of the first civilians to land in France after D-Day. His job was to organise these leave centres.

Below Towards the end of the Second World War, large numbers of troops were arriving in France, whilst awaiting their return to Britain. Billy set up a number of NAAFIs in the area which became known as the 'leave' area. He also opened eight clubs in Belgium, Holland and Germany.

Most pictures of Billy were taken whilst working on the camps or during specific events. This posed photograph was taken at his office in Oxford Street, London. The pictures on the wall record some of the key moments in his life.

Here we see Billy with Winifred West, his secretary, who worked for him from 1949 until his retirement in 1968. She continued working for the company until 1977 when she retired. Billy received many accolades during his life, including an MBE in 1945 for services during the war and a Knighthood in 1964 for his services to the church. In 1972 he was awarded the Variety Club's Humanitarian Award and was named an 'International Philanthropist Extraordinary'. He donated large sums of money annually to provide homes for children, initiated schemes for the welfare of young people and supported other diverse charitable causes.

Billy Butlin stands proudly outside his Oxford Street headquarters in 1968, raising his hat to the company on his retirement day. He remained as a consultant but was reported to have said that he was never consulted! One cannot imagine his thoughts on retirement from a job which had become the realisation of a lifetime's ambition.

Following his death on 12 June 1980, Sir William Butlin was buried in the cemetery of St John's Church on the island of Jersey. His funeral was attended by numerous people he had met through his camps, the world of entertainment, and the various charities he had supported throughout his life. This truly great man is recognised for his involvement with holiday camps and amusement parks and rumour has it that he chose his final resting place to ensure easy access for members of the public to view his unique gravestone with the story of his life engraved into the marble. A showman to the end!

two

Holiday Camps

The Butlin Empire had many different facets, the most prolific and well known being the 'holiday camps', as they were originally known, but which are now referred to as 'resorts' to conform to the modern perception of holidays.

Billy visited Skegness in 1927 in search of a suitable site for an amusement park. He recognised the potential of a vacant spot of land and the first of his camps opened here in 1936. It was to mark a change in direction for British holidays. 'A week's holiday for a week's pay' became the catchphrase in the early publicity. Following the successful opening of Skegness, he made plans for a second camp at Clacton, which opened in 1938 at a cost of £100,000. Early season visitors would number only 400 a week, rising to 6,000 in peak weeks, with the majority being from the London area. He was careful to position his camps within 200 miles of a large populated area, and aimed to provide entertainment and facilities which would ensure a return the following year. In 1939, war put an end to holidays of this nature but these camps were used by the Armed Forces, including the partially built camps at Filey, Ayr and Pwllheli.

At the end of the Second World War, the camps were returned to Billy Butlin, renovated and quickly reopened for their original purpose. Five camps were now in operation and in 1948 he had embarked on the Mosney camp in Eire, where they preferred the name 'holiday village'. The numbers of holidaymakers increased through the 1950s, and in the 1960s demand saw the number of camps increase with the building of camps at Bognor Regis, Minehead and Barry Island, the ninth and last camp to be built, in 1966. The nine camps varied in capacity from 4,000 to 12,000 weekly and it was in 1963 that figures in excess of one million were recorded. With this success came the need to increase the size of the earlier camps and considerable expansion occurred for a number of years. However, the advent of 'package holidays abroad' seriously affected the demand for UK holidays.

In 1972, following a number of take-over attempts, Butlin Holidays Ltd was sold to the Rank Organisation, who invested heavily in updating the camps to cater for the modern trends now expected. Within a decade, some camps became expendable and in the 1980s Mosney, Clacton, Filey and later Barry Island were closed. The remaining sites were re-launched as 'holiday worlds'. Visitor numbers increased and by 1992 the peak figures of the 1970s were achieved. In 1997 Rank, who also owned Haven Holidays (mainly caravan parks), transferred the Ayr and Pwllheli camps to the Haven brand and invested heavily in the three remaining camps at Bognor Regis, Minehead and Skegness, which continue to operate under the Butlin banner to this day. In 2000, when investment failed to gain the expected return, the whole Rank Holidays' Division, which now included Warner Holidays, was sold to Bourne Leisure Ltd. During 2010 the annual figures of guests and day visitors for the three remaining resorts was in the region of 480,000 for Bognor Regis, 620,000 for Skegness and 550,000 for Minehead, thus giving a total of 1,650,000 people visiting the company.

Bourne Leisure Ltd made, and are still making, enormous changes to the three sites, which are now known as 'family entertainment resorts' but still carry the Butlin banner. Chalets are fast disappearing and hotels are springing up on parts of the sites along with spas and the opportunity of timeshare. If Billy returned today there is no doubt he would feel satisfied as his original aim is still evident but with a new and modern interpretation.

The following pages feature the various camps in the order in which they opened (Skegness 1936, Clacton 1938, Filey 1946, Pwllheli & Ayr 1947, Mosney 1948, Bognor Regis 1960, Minehead 1962, and Barry Island 1966).

Just one month before he opened his first camp this advertisement appeared in the *Sheffield Telegraph*, announcing the arrival of Butlin's Holiday Camp. The camp opened on 11 April 1936 and is one of only three still operating today. Between 1987 and 1998 it was renamed Funcoast World, before returning to the well-known 'Butlin's.'

Campers of To-day: Two of the Four Thousand on Holiday at Skegness
In the old days, camping meant boiling a kettle outside a tent in a meadow. There was privacy, but little comfort. In the vast new holiday camps, such as this one at Skegness, you can have it both ways. You sleep in your own separate chalet; but have all the comforts and amusements at your door.

HOLIDAY CAMP

Everyone was excited about the new concept of a holiday camp; no more draughty tents or camp fires. Instead you had your own separate chalet with all its comforts, and entertainments right on your doorstep. The advertising stated there was running water – however, it was only cold. Hot water was available along each chalet line, as shown here by two early morning campers at the outside tap at Skegness in 1939. Each chalet had a large enamel jug in the chalet for this purpose.

CHALETS. BUTLINS HOLIDAY CAMP SKEGNESS.

Two hundred acres of former sugar beet and turnip fields at Skegness was the first site for Billy. It accommodated 1,000 people and cost £100,000 to build. Six hundred detached chalets were constructed in lines, each surrounded by picturesque flower borders, at the end of which were toilet and bathroom blocks.

'Goodnight Campers." Chalet Interior.
Butlin's Holiday Camp, Skegness.   "Empire View." 022-415.

The wardrobe was a three-sided wooden cupboard with 'yacht' fabric curtains in front and matching curtains at the windows. In later years a blue candlewick bedspread was provided with a 'B' embroidered on it, and sheets being either pink or blue. Here a rug covers the varnished wooden floorboards but these were not generally available.

An Elizabethan chalet was built at Skegness in 1936. These 10ft by 10ft chalets were constructed of a timber frame with in-fill consisting of chicken wire covered with cement. Designed by Billy himself, each chalet cost approximately £10 to build. The one remaining original chalet was for many years a gardener's shed at Skegness. In July 1968 it became a Grade II listed building and still stands today as an attraction for holidaymakers visiting Skegness.

In 1939 on arrival at Skegness, campers were directed to reception to purchase a book of tea vouchers and Butlin's early morning tea service would do the rest. Each morning (early) the blue and yellow tea trolley announced its arrival by the ringing of musical bells. On production of a tea voucher you would receive your cuppa. An article in a 1939 brochure stated, 'the tea was that delicious, reviving coppery brown tea, just like mother makes.' At odd hours between meals a trolley would be taken around the chalet lines with lemonade and ice creams.

BUTLIN'S SKEGNESS HOLIDAY CAMP.

Campers on holiday at Butlin's were encouraged to enrol in the Keep Fit Teams and displays were held weekly on each camp. The ladies were then invited to continue in clubs set up in the bigger towns and cities and from these came the large demonstrations seen at football grounds around the country. The whole programme was put together by Captain T.J. Bond, who was Director of Physical Recreation for Butlin's from 1936 until the mid-1960s.

Here's every Good Wish for a Happy & Prosperous New Year

BUTLINS SKEGNESS

1937

from the Staff

Billy recognised that success lay with good advertising and although his camps were closed during the winter months, he continued to attract the holidaymaker's attention by producing things such as this 1937 New Year postcard, which featured his management team. The message on this pre-printed postcard read: 'and by the way we've got some surprises for you at Skegness for the summer ... Still bigger and better entertainment ... We're working hard on some pleasant additions ... Still you'll be seeing ... p.s. don't forget our Reunion Dance 1st Jan. Olympia London'.

Luxuriously designed dining halls

Above With the popularity of Butlin's holidays growing, Skegness was greatly enlarged for the 1939 season. One of the many new buildings was a dining room named Gloucester House, the opening ceremony of which was performed by the Duchess of Gloucester. All of Butlin's dining rooms were thereafter named after Dukedoms Kent, Gloucester, Windsor, Edinburgh, York and Connaught.

Left Joe Velich, one of the initial members of staff at Skegness, was a well-known face featured on postcards and in brochures. He enjoyed posing with campers and celebrities alike around the site and regularly acted as the referee at weekly boxing tournaments.

Seen here with Billy on a social cycle is Godfrey Winn, on one of his many visits to Butlin's. Godfrey was a camper at Butlin's before the war and returned in 1947. He proudly boasted of having ten Butlin Badges. He once wrote in his weekly column in a national Sunday newspaper, 'I have just had my own first taste of the most important social experiment of our times, and have met the happiest crowd of holidaymakers to be found anywhere at the seaside.'

A boating regatta was held every week on the long boating lake at Skegness. Here we see one of the races about to start. Activities, games and competitions were always important on the camps, allowing both parents and children to enjoy their holiday.

Fun and games with Redcoat Freddy Davis. Freddy went on to become known as 'Parrotface' when he blossomed as a stage and television entertainer. He joined the Skegness Entertainments Department in 1958 and received free board and lodgings with a wage of £6 10s. He was also given his red coat, two nylon shirts, tie, white trousers and a plastic mac.

The Skegness Security Team outside the Gaiety Theatre, c. 1970. As there is such a big line-up one would presume there was an important visit about to occur. From left to right: Bill Wragg, Bill Lucas, -?-, Jock McGee, -?-, -?-, Geoff Kent, -?-.

READING ROOM, BUTLINS HOLIDAY CAMP, SKEGNESS.

In the 1930s and '40s a quiet area was available for campers to relax with papers and magazines. This large room, with Lloyd Loom furniture and potted palms, set exactly the right atmosphere for a break between more hectic activities.

MODERN COCKTAIL BAR, BUTLINS HOLIDAY CAMP, SKEGNESS.

Whilst travelling, Billy was always looking for new ideas. Here he introduced a modern trend, a cocktail bar that he had seen on a trip to America.

Phone : Skegness 490

The **Butlin** THEATRE SKEGNESS

SHOWPLACE OF THE COAST

Open to the Public   **Free Car Park**

The theatre at the Skegness camp was bought by Billy after the British Empire Exhibition in Glasgow, which was attended by twelve million people between March and December 1938. He had the prefabricated building dismantled, transported and re-erected and then added bricks to the façade. It was adjacent to the Ingoldmells Hotel at his Skegness Camp and he named it the Gaiety Theatre. It had a seating capacity of 1,750 and boasted that it was the largest air-conditioned theatre in Europe at that time.

The Butlin Gaiety Theatre was very well known both in Lincolnshire and beyond. In addition to campers and local residents, coaches brought large numbers of people wishing to see the top acts of the day. In 1946 Billy engaged the San Carlo Opera Company to appear at Skegness in an attempt to bring culture to people who were unable to travel to London.

Right The Ingoldmells Hotel was built adjacent to the camp in 1939, when the camp itself was enlarged due to increased numbers of visitors. During the Second World War, part of the hotel was used as an Officers' Mess. Following a serious fire on 5 June 1974, which burnt down the Princess and Reception buildings, the perimeter fence was removed and the Ingoldmells building was encompassed as part of the camp, thus replacing those facilities destroyed by fire.

INGOLDMELLS HOTEL.
BUTLINS HOLIDAY CAMP SKEGNESS.

Below The new hotel was given up-to-the-minute interior décor. In spite of the need to accommodate large numbers, the Palm Court Lounge still had a casual, relaxed atmosphere.

INGOLDMELLS PALM COURT
BUTLINS HOLIDAY CAMP SKEGNESS

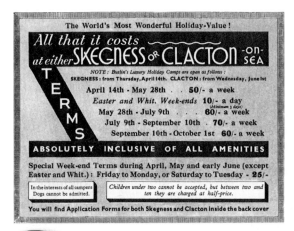

The World's Most Wonderful Holiday-Value!

All that it costs
at either SKEGNESS or CLACTON -on-SEA

NOTE : Butlin's Luxury Holiday Camps are open as follows :
SKEGNESS : from Thursday, April 14th. CLACTON : from Wednesday, June 1st

T E R M S

April 14th - May 28th . . **50/-** a week
Easter and Whit. Week-ends **10/-** a day
(Minimum 3 days)
May 28th - July 9th . . . **60/-** a week
July 9th - September 10th . **70/-** a week
September 10th - October 1st **60/-** a week

ABSOLUTELY   INCLUSIVE   OF   ALL   AMENITIES

Special Week-end Terms during April, May and early June (except
Easter and Whit.) : Friday to Monday, or Saturday to Tuesday - **25/-**

| In the interests of all campers Dogs cannot be admitted. | Children under two cannot be accepted, but between two and ten they are charged at half-price. |

You will find Application Forms for both Skegness and Clacton inside the back cover

In 1938 the Government launched their Holidays with Pay Act, which coincided with the opening of the second Butlin's holiday camp at Clacton-on-Sea, Essex, on 11 June. The Act guaranteed industrial workers at least a week's paid holiday each year. The cost of a week's holiday at Clacton was equivalent to the average industrial wage of 70s. Sadly, due to the outbreak of war, the Clacton camp only completed two seasons, closing on 4 September 1939. It reopened after hostilities ceased on 6 April 1946 before finally closing its doors on 18 October 1983. The former site is now a housing estate with no reference to its Butlin's history.

The Jolly Roger, Butlin's Holiday Camp, Clacton-on-Sea. 'Empire View' 120.

This postcard of the 'Jolly Roger' bar at Clacton is postmarked September 1938 and carries the message, 'Having a great time here, weather is perfect, very warm and sunny. Entertainment and competitions start at 9 o'clock and finish at 11.30 p.m. There is no need to go outside the camp for anything and there are 1,400 people here this week.' This was exactly the sort of publicity that Billy was always looking for.

New arrivals at the Clacton camp would pass the outdoor swimming pool to check-in at the Main Reception Building, top right of the picture. After the war, catering at home or on holiday was difficult as rationing continued until the early 1950s. On arrival at reception, holidaymakers would be required to hand in their ration books and the appropriate vouchers would be taken to cover food supplied by Butlin's. One lady who visited the camp as a child remembers saving her sweet coupons in a tin, ready for her holidays.

The Clacton shopping centre after the camp had re-opened post war. When war was declared on 3 September 1939, Billy was asked by the War Office how quickly he could close down the Clacton camp as it was to be requisitioned for the army. Within a week the Army Pioneer Corps was installed and Butlin's had to reimburse all the campers who were booked for the rest of the season.

In the early years, chalets had no heating or hot water. Billy ordered a supply of dustbins, punched holes around the sides, fitted a red electric light bulb inside to make them look like braziers, and placed them around the main buildings. Early advertising in the years after the war stated, 'Sleep in private chalets designed for two, three, or four persons, with fitted wash basins and running water. The beds have interior sprung mattresses. Hot baths are always available at the toilet/bathroom blocks located along the chalet line'. All this was a far cry from the smaller camps that were springing up around Britain and camping under canvas!

The Viennese Ballroom was a popular place to visit. Competitions for children and adults alike were held there during the day, after which it became a modern dance venue for the evening. A separate ballroom was available for old-time dancers and in later years, when rock'n'roll became popular, yet another ballroom was provided. For those who preferred to watch television, two rooms with cinema-type seating were assigned, one for BBC and the other for ITV or 'Commercial' as it was then known. Now, of course, every chalet or hotel room has its own multi-channel television.

BUTLIN'S CLACTON
The Reception Hall

To encourage saving for future holidays, Billy introduced a scheme whereby stamps to the value of 2s 6d could be purchased from reception or by post from Head Office. A full book of stamps totalled £10. Reception was a very busy venue on Saturdays as this was the change-over day for most holidaymakers. For a nominal cost, luncheon packs were available for guests to take on their return journey home.

Campers had many opportunities to engage in new activities on holiday and here a group of young people are enjoying roller-skating around the camp in 1953. Roller-skating rinks were provided on every camp and over the years many Canadian ice hockey professionals were employed as Redcoat skating instructors. Skates were provided free of charge and it only required the chalet key to act as a deposit. From left to right are: Dave ?, Eileen Woodward, Mr and Mrs Woodward, Sid ?, Jean Warren, Mary Woodward, George Sayers, Sylvia Gunner and seated is Fritz.

Ladies taking part in one of the numerous competitions held throughout the week. From left to right are: Sylvia Gunner, Mary Woodward, Jean Warren, -?-. On the left of the picture is a sign promoting the Festival of Britain. Billy also supported the National Playing Fields Association, whose patron, HRH Prince Phillip, accepted an annual donation from the proceeds of a car raffle held weekly on every camp throughout the season.

Butlin photographers took pictures of all the diners every week and these could be purchased as souvenirs. Similarly, pictures were taken of the participants engaging in all activities, as well as general crowd scenes, and all these were displayed in the Photographic Shop and endorsed with a code number to simplify the purchase of a picture. Pictured here are Margaret Gunner, Janet Stephens, Dot ? and Sheila ? enjoying their evening meal at Clacton in 1953.

BUTLIN'S CLACTON
Rock and Twist Ballroom

As dance styles changed, it became necessary to provide separate facilities to cater for the rock'n' twist (later, rock'n'roll) and the more strict tempo modern, and old time. Dancers became irate because of the many collisions on the dance floor and the introduction of designated ballrooms solved the problem.

The original Clacton camp opened with a capacity of only 400 but this increased rapidly to 3,000. Eventually the camp held 6,000, following an enlargement in 1955. When it closed in 1984 there were 900 seasonal staff and nearly 100 permanent staff.

The entire staff of Clacton in 1956. In 1955 the *Illustrated* magazine featured a full colour, double-page photograph of all the staff at Clacton. Butlin's used the picture for a mini-brochure early the following year and in view of its advertising value it was repeated at all camps the following season.

This Clacton walkway was used by campers to reach the entertainment areas from their accommodation. To brighten up this area, Spanish-style ends were added to the end of the chalet lines in the late 1950s and early '60s. Besides making them look more interesting, the doors were used to hide unsightly electrical boxes and cables. By the 1980s the site began to look outdated and, after failing to make a profit for three years, it was closed in October 1983. In 1984 it was sold and renamed Atlas Park. Shortly afterwards, it was demolished and is now a housing estate and coach park. It is still sadly missed!

Architect's Impression of Butlin's Luxury Holiday Camp
Filey Bay
Opening Whitsun 1940
Occupying an Area of over 190 Acres

This advertisement appeared in a Skegness brochure prior to the Second World War. Billy purchased 190 acres and paid a total of £12,000 to start his new camp, which was due to open at Whitsun 1940. During the war it was used by the RAF to train personnel and became known as RAF Humnanby Moor. The camp reopened to holidaymakers on 2 June 1945 and the centre finally closed on 18 October 1983.

A Happy Holiday awai... you at
Butlin's
439, OXFORD ST, LONDON, W.1
Free Brochure from
A.7271

The Filey camp was different to many of the other camps as it was on several levels and had a large number of brick buildings along avenues. The camp opened with accommodation for 1,500 campers, which quickly rose to 5,000, and at the height of its popularity it covered 400 acres and could accommodate 10,000 campers.

Filey camp was situated near the Scarborough railway line and a short branch line was built to link to the camp. It was opened on 10 May 1947 and here we see eight girls from the Butlin's Ladies Aerobics team at the opening ceremony. Billy liaised with the railway companies so that all campers going to his camps at Pwllheli, Ayr and Mosney, where they had their own station, would be sent a 'Plan your travel' leaflet.

'Here come the girls!' Filey camp railway station braces itself at the start of the Wakes Weeks holiday. In 1958 British Railways advertised that they carried over 250,000 passengers annually to a Butlin's holiday centre. However, due to the rise in car ownership, rail travel dwindled and in 1977 the camp station was closed by British Rail.

Right This, possibly metallic, horse was obviously being enjoyed by this young girl. Many images from Butlin's carried either the logo across the bottom corner or, in some cases, a white circle with a number to enable campers to order their own copy.

Below Many features of the Butlin's camps contained wording, so that any pictures taken could act as publicity for the company. This mother and son were enjoying the chairlift which took campers down to the sea. The chairlift was opened in 1961.

In 1957 Charlie arrived at Filey after a five-day journey from Ayr camp. He was transported in a lorry and the journey was so slow it was said that he could have walked the journey in the same time. He was reputed to be the 'largest elephant in Europe' at the time.

The Parliamentary Bar at Filey was an exact replica of the one at Westminster in London. In his younger years Billy wanted to enter the film industry, and soon became friends with Pinewood Studios, who would supply him with 'leftover or used' sets. He also had an arrangement whereby he took over the Oxford Street lights in London after each Christmas to use at his camps.

At one time, one of the colourful features of Butlin's was the flying of national flags at the front of each holiday centre. They were raised daily at 10 a.m. by a member of the security department. Whilst Sylvia was at Ayr she saw the flags lowered to half mast as a mark of respect when the children's entertainer, Uncle Ray, died in the summer of 1972.

The area which later became the boating lake was in fact the parade ground used by the troops during the Second World War. We will never know how many of these men returned years later to Filey for a Butlin holiday.

In addition to the numerous weekly holidaymakers' competitions, there were the occasional staff competitions too, which senior managers would be called upon to judge. Pictured here in 1976, from left to right, are: Revd J. Rhodes (padre), Shirley Lewis (nursery manager), Terry Stanley (Head Office main catering), Mrs Anne Smith (Filey personnel manager) and standing is Mr Pete Scrace (catering manager).

These large, quiet lounges were a distinctive feature of Butlin's during the 1960s and '70s. They were a place where guests could read the newspaper or a book, look at the views or have quick nap after lunch. These were an updated version of the quiet reading rooms of the 1930s and '40s with their Lloyd Loom furniture. Unfortunately Filey closed in 1985 and, despite various purchases, it never became a major entertainment facility.

In August 1963 Billy (by now Sir William Butlin MBE) hosted a visit to Pwllheli by Her Majesty Queen Elizabeth II together with His Royal Highness Prince Philip. The royal visit to North Wales was seen to be the forerunner of preparations for the Investiture of Prince Charles at Caernarvon Castle. It is thought that the opportunity to visit the Butlin camp at Pwllheli was prompted by Prince Philip, who started his naval career there during the Second World War when the camp was a navy training base known as HMS *Glendower*. After introductions to senior executives, the Queen and Prince Philip toured the camp in an open-topped Land Rover, acknowledging thousands of holidaymakers lining the route. A far different atmosphere to when Prince Philip was first here!

Building of the Pwllheli Holiday Camp had only recently commenced when the Second World War was announced and within three weeks, 8,000 naval ratings arrived to begin training and to live in Bell tents as pictured. It opened as a holiday camp in 1947, becoming very popular with holidaymakers from the north west of England. From 1990 to 1998, to conform to the Holiday Worlds marketing policy, it was known as Starcoast World.

Originally built as detached units, in about 1956/7 it was decided to modernise these and add en-suite bathroom and toilet facilities between each chalet. Hot water was piped to every chalet at this time. In August 1966 Pwllheli became the only camp, before or since, to pass 12,000 holidaymakers in one week. In 1998 Pwllheli lost its Butlin banner and was transferred to another of the Rank Holidays Division, Haven Holidays, and is known now as Hafon-y-Mor.

BUTLIN'S PWLLHELI
The Riding School

The ropeway (chairlift) at Pwllheli opened in March 1960 and carried passengers along the one-and-a-half-mile route, providing stunning views over the camp, Snowdonia and Harlech Bay. According to a 1962 programme, it carried 600 campers per hour, rose to over 100ft, and travelled at a speed of 200 yards per minute. Adjacent to the camp was a riding school, where campers could join groups and ride to the headlands.

This picture shows children enjoying the ever-popular donkey rides, which were available on the South Camp playing field. These donkeys were provided by Don Trapnell of Weston-super-Mare. At Pwllheli and Ayr the donkeys were in-situ for the whole season whilst at the other camps teams of donkeys would visit for a couple of days each week. Campers had to pay 20p for donkey rides unless they took part in the weekly Donkey Derby.

For many in 1959, sitting in a lounger chair by the outdoor swimming pool and looking across to the majesty of Mount Snowdon in the distance was a great way to spend the day. The same pool saw huge crowds for the weekly Swimming Gala, where various swimming and diving competitions were compered by Ron Stanway.

From an early 1950s' brochure we find that 'the diet at Butlin's was reinforced in every way possible with un-rationed foods. Meals were served at separate tables for four by waiters and waitresses. Electrically heated containers called "Jacksons" ensured that the food reached the table as hot as when it left the model kitchens.' This view of the dining hall is one that is fondly remembered by guests, together with the cheers that arose when a plate was dropped. In 1966 it was advertised that 'you do no more for yourself than you would at any first class hotel. Mother gets a real rest at Butlin's.'

This picture was taken following the disastrous fire at Pwllheli in the summer of 1971, when the entire Gaiety Building, which covered over an acre of ground, was destroyed. This very busy building encompassed two theatres, two restaurants, two coffee bars, three licensed bars, the modern ballroom, numerous shops, a quiet lounge, the entertainment department offices, table tennis room and snooker room. In November 1971, the first girders of the new building are seen here being toasted by, from left to right: Ron Stanway (visiting executive from Head Office, who supplied the beer!), 'Darkie' Roberts (Maintenance Manager), 'Rocky' Mason (Entertainment Manager), Bob Thompson (Assistant General Manager), -?- (site contractor), Leonard Watkins (Camp General Manager).

These new two-storey 'A-frame' chalets were introduced at Pwllheli in the 1980s for use by the self-catering campers and were known as 'Snowdon Lodges'.

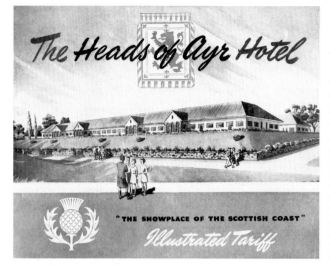

Advertising for Ayr camp in the early 1950s stated that, 'By the Heads of Ayr, in the Robert Burns country, this charming holiday village is only 30 miles from Glasgow. The actual Heads of Ayr hotel was at road level and the camp was reached after descending a short hill. It provides all the pleasure for which Butlin's are renowned, besides its own distinctly Scottish atmosphere, and is an ideal centre from which to visit such priceless landmarks as the Wallace Tower, Ayr, Brig O'Doon and the Auld Haunted Kirk.'

The Ayr camp was opened on 17 May 1947 by Sir Harry Lauder and eventually closed on 1 November 1998 as a Butlin's holiday camp. Initially, pipers would march around the camp to wake the campers prior to breakfast; latterly this task was carried out by Radio Butlin. There was an old railway line running through this area and plans were soon implemented to reopen this line for the convenience of the campers, a service that continued until the end of 1968.

During the war, the site was named HMS *Scotia*. In July 1985, Ken Hudson, Camp General Manager
(left) and Gibson McDonald, leader of the Kyle & Carrick District Council, unveiled a plaque
to record this memorable event. The Royal Naval Training Establishment was in existence from
January 1942 until January 1948. Some of the trainees went first to HMS *Royal Arthur* (Skegness)
and then transferred to Ayr to complete their training before final examinations. Many Royal Naval
Commandos were briefed and trained here before storming the Normandy beaches.

Advertising brochures over the years have taken many forms. In 1947 this particular issue for Ayr was produced with sepia pictures in this ornate surround. Each centre had a unique brochure with their particular information, rather than today's standardised but very colourful format.

This 1954 Campers Committee Group photograph is one of thousands that would have been taken on the camps. However, this one is special because Bobbie Butlin is in the picture working as a Redcoat. From left to right, back row: Don Cook, -?-, 'Prof' Davis. In the middle row we have Tom 'Knocker' White (far left) and Bobbie Butlin (far right). On the retirement of his father in 1968, Bobbie became Chairman and MD of the company, retiring in 1984. He died in December 2008.

Opposite In 1972 the Ayr centre staff asked if they could produce a talent show as part of the staff entertainment programme. The resultant show was performed in front of the guests in the main theatre. From left to right, back row: Joe Cuthbert, Moira Paterson, Jim Kidd, Charlie Taylor, Janice Law, Tom McLaughlin, Teresa Joyce, Saz Bateman, Joe Campbell (who compered the show), Sylvia Endacott. Front row: Paul Tague, Ricki Wilson, Pat McShannon. All the participants in the show worked in non-entertainment departments at the centre.

All sections of the company have staff that operate behind the scenes and never come into contact with the guests. In 1971 Sylvia was personnel manager at Ayr in Scotland and is seen here with her staff. The personnel department was involved in the recruitment of most of the staff that helped to make guests' holidays more pleasant. They were, from left to right, back row: –?–, –?–, Sylvia Endacott, Morah ?, Mrs Allardyce (welfare officer), Mrs Shakespeare (welfare officer). Front row: Peter McLaughlin (assistant personnel manager) and Mr Ross (welfare officer).

There was a Beachcomber Bar at most holiday centres during the 1960s and '70s. It is alleged that Billy chose the name after visiting a bar in the Mayfair Hotel in London. The aim of these bars was to create the illusion of a tropical island paradise, complete with exotic cocktails and staff in grass skirts. You were also able to 'see' a volcanic eruption followed by a tropical storm. Some were advertised as 'Polynesian-style Beachcomber Bars' – they were for adults only.

In 1971 the Late Night Cabarets were held in the Beachcomber Bar and Jimmy Logan would regularly appear at the Ayr Centre, he was a great favourite with the Scottish audience of the time.

In 1959, the popular singing star Eve Boswell accompanied Billy when he opened the Rope Railway at Ayr. It was a great success and by 1962 they had been installed at Pwllheli, Skegness and Filey. The installation by the British Ropeway Engineering Co. Ltd cost £50,000 and was considered to be an outstanding feat of engineering.

This photograph shows the management team at Ayr camp in June 1973. From left to right, back row: Neville Mason, (catering), Bob Fairburn, (accommodation), Jim Warhurst (camp general manager), Vic Styles (administration), J. Smith (maintenance), Harry Cuff (entertainment), Joe Cuthbert (assistant personnel manager), Gareth Rees (accountant), Rosemary Fidley (secretary). Front row: John Kane (stores), Ian Campbell (deputy camp general manager), John Townend (shops and bars), Peter Gray (deputy catering manager). This was the team with whom Sylvia worked for four years before moving to Bognor Regis. Many members of management worked for the company over a long period of time, or moved around the company to gain promotion.

Mosney Holiday Village, County Meath, was opened in 1948 on 200 acres of a former country estate on the east coast of Southern Ireland. Being adjacent to the Dublin/Belfast railway line, a camp station was created for the benefit of campers. At its peak the camp could accommodate 2,800 campers and 4,000 day visitors. In 1978 it was reported that over 50,000 guests had used the station. Although still profitable, Butlin's were looking to downsize and the site was advertised for sale in 1980. It was sold as a going concern in 1982 and continued much the same under the name of 'Mosney Holiday Centre'. By 2000, with dwindling numbers and recruitment problems, the site was sold to the government, who turned it into an accommodation centre for asylum seekers.

Irish campers were very proud to have this label on their luggage. Butlin's occupies a unique place in Irish social history. In 2010 there was a petition to the Irish Heritage Authorities to preserve and maintain the original Butlin buildings as the last remaining major British holiday camp that is largely unchanged. One possible long-term plan is for it to become a 'retro'-themed holiday camp or a working museum.

Mosney in the 1960s had an open and uncrowded feel and featured more simple activities, as seen here. There were fewer amusements than at other camps. It was said to be more 'up market' and referred to itself as a 'village' rather than a camp, aiming itself more towards young couples.

Mosney always had an air of peace and tranquillity. Holidaymakers appeared happy to relax and enjoy their surroundings and even the staff seemed to have more time to talk with visitors.

At one time, it was reported that eight out of ten Irish families had a link with the camp either as holidaymakers or staff. Each year more than 6,000 children from around the country visited to take part in the Community Games. This event was held for over twenty-five years and Mosney was the only place in Ireland that had sufficient beds for this June event, which was organised by the Lions Club, and also provided holidays for local people.

The Butlin Riding School is seen here assembling ready to trot along the leafy country lanes of County Meath and enjoy the beauty of the countryside. It was also possible to have a quiet canter on the Strand and special tuition was available for beginners. The not so energetic campers could take a ride through the camp on an authentic Irish jaunting cart.

Angela Kelly, chief hostess and 'Irish' Jesson, Redcoat entertainer, at the Carlton Cinema in Dublin in 1965. This was just one of hundreds of exhibitions held through the winter months in which Redcoats would promote the company. All forms of advertising were used by the company in the days before the internet.

Billy first arrived in Bognor Regis in 1931 with a recreational centre on the promenade. Around the top of the building was emblazoned 'Our True Intent Is All For Your Delight'. The building housed a twenty-six-car dodgem track, a mirror maze, rifle range, juvenile rides, laughing clowns, housey housey, and the largest display of slot machines seen on the coast at that time. Pictured is one of his tokens.

This advertisement in the *Bognor Regis Post* appeared when Billy was first making his name in the entertainment world in the late 1930s. 'Hurrah! It's Butlin's' became one of the slogans of the day.

Right A zoo and aquarium was opened by Billy in 1933 along the promenade. It was entered through a high rock façade as shown in the picture. Local advertisements claimed that black, brown and polar bears were to be seen alongside leopards, hyenas, pelicans, kangaroos and monkeys. A special attraction was 'Togo the Snake King', who gave frequent shows in the snake pit erected in the centre of the zoo.

Below In the late 1950s, the Bognor Regis Town Council decided that they would prefer the Butlin's seafront facilities to move to an available area of land at the far end of the promenade. There were 500 staff involved in building the camp who were paid 8s 6d per hour to construct the 1,600 chalets. It cost £15 per week full board at the centre where they planted 2,000 trees and 20,000 rose bushes.

Left This 'shell' eventually became the main reception building with offices above. Following the closure of many of the centres and hotels, the upper floor was transformed into a call centre for the new owners, Bourne Leisure. In 2005 this moved to Hemel Hempstead, the new headquarters of this major entertainments company. Between 1987 and 1998 it was known as Southcoast World and is still operational today.

Below The Bognor Regis holiday centre opened on 2 July 1960 and had 30,000 campers that season. In April 1999 it was renamed the Family Entertainment Resort. There have been a number of major changes to the centre, with the demolition of older buildings and also the construction of many new and exciting areas of the centre, including two superb hotels with a third hotel construction starting in 2010.

Here we see the construction of the indoor swimming pool, with its distinctive glass windows. The local press commented that 'Bognor Butlin's will be the best ever' when they reported that 'stubby millionaire Billy Butlin, surrounded by the heads of his empire, motored into Bognor Regis for a personal inspection of the overgrown stretch of the seafront which will give rise to his £3,000,000 holiday camp.'

The indoor swimming pool proved very popular with campers and was also welcomed by locals when Butlin's opened throughout the winter months as a 'Winter Social Club'. According to a 1961 programme, these pools included 'imitation parrots and monkeys swinging from perches, jets of water sparkling in the air as they sprung from the pool sides, lending an exotic touch to a scene of incomparable beauty.'

This was the popular beach gate, which allowed campers to go onto the promenade, the beach and into the town of Bognor Regis. It was also the entrance for the day visitors and it was here, in Bognor Regis, that they had one of the highest numbers of day visitors into any centre.

During the 1970s the Lawn Tennis Association (LTA) wanted to be seen to promote tennis to the wider public, and approached Harold Vinter of Butlin's to enquire about the use of the camps. Arrangements were made, tiered seating was ordered and the LTA party arrived by helicopter as arranged. LTA teenagers were flown in and professional players coached them and concluded the session with exhibition sets. The names of professionals were guaranteed to bring the Butlin's holidaymakers along in great numbers. Australian and Wimbledon champions, Rod Laver and Ken Rosewall, were great favourites and immensely popular, as was the British Ladies Champion, Ann Jones. Bobbie Butlin is seen here at Bognor Regis on one of the promotional days.

Early in 1963, Billy met Colonel Sir Michael Ansell on a train to Devon and had a discussion about show jumping. A meeting was later held with the British Show Jumping Association to determine whether there was sufficient room for spectators and of course parking for the horseboxes. Finally, it was agreed that events could be held at the camps, much to the enjoyment of guests for over twenty years.

In 1999 Butlin's undertook a major revamp of the Bognor Regis centre and when it reopened, the Skyline Pavilion was designed to provide a weatherproof venue for a range of restaurants, shops and entertainments. Singer Ronan Keating was at the Bognor Regis Resort to open this new £40 million mini-dome, alleged to be as big as the football pitch at Wembley Stadium. These pavilions created an exciting skyline and still exist on the three remaining centres.

Following many years of chalets and external hotels in other resorts, the new owners have decided to move forward and here we see the Shoreline Hotel, opened in August 2005 and named after a Bognor Regis hotel of the past. At that time the Bognor Regis Resort could accommodate up to 5,000 guests with 300,000 visiting in a year. This new hotel has 160 rooms and can accommodate up to 640 guests.

Postcards have always formed a part of the Butlin's advertising machine, but occasionally they produced more descriptive cards and this is one of the authors' favourites. It was posted in 1964 with the message stating 'plenty to do and see here'. Sylvia worked here in 1969, when she joined Butlin's as an assistant personnel manager.

1 An invitation printed in a brochure in 1955.

2 Billy fitted a revolving stage in the Gaiety Theatre of every camp … each one was larger in diameter than that at the London Palladium.

3 This 1960s slogan encapsulated Billy's dream.

4 The boating lake at Bognor Regis was replaced by these gardens and water features.

5 An advertisement in a 1965 programme promoting *The People*, a newspaper which could be purchased from the onsite newsagent.

6 Happy, smiling campers always featured on the annual postcard.

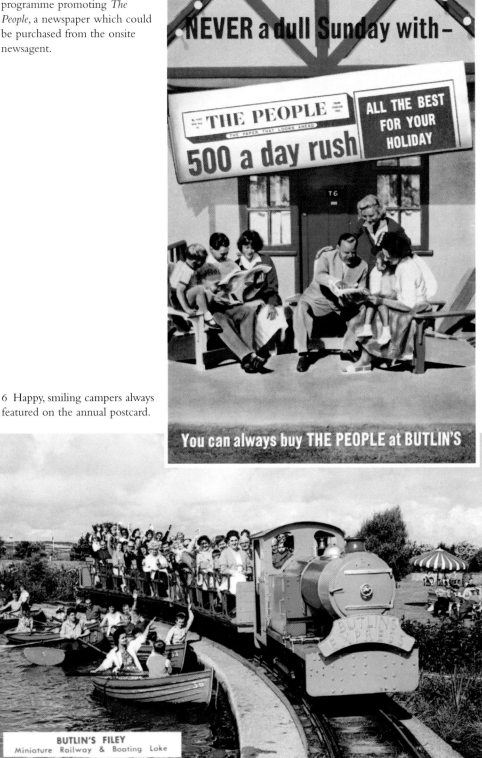

NEVER a dull Sunday with—

THE PEOPLE

500 a day rush

ALL THE BEST FOR YOUR HOLIDAY

You can always buy THE PEOPLE at BUTLIN'S

BUTLIN'S FILEY
Miniature Railway & Boating Lake

7 The Butlin's holiday village by the sea in the 1950s.

8 The exotic interior of one of the famous Beachcomber Bars, complete with grass-skirted waitresses.

Opposite from top
9 The words may change, but the idea remains the same.
10 The formal swimming lanes at Wonderwest World Ayr were replaced by flumes, waves and fountains.

11 Sun, sand and sea – all the ingredients necessary for a relaxing and enjoyable holiday with children.

12 Guests may now own a little piece of Butlin's by purchasing a Blue Skies timeshare apartment at the Minehead resort.

13 Billy invites you to his new luxury holiday camps.

14 Guests enjoying their holiday in the New England-style accommodation, which is unique to Skegness.

15 A 1950s programme inviting families to experience a fun-filled holiday.

16 A new concept for Butlin's: a hotel with a spa. The Ocean Hotel opened in 2009 as the second hotel at the Bognor Regis Resort.

Here in Minehead we see the outdoor pool and the monorail. It is reported that Billy was at Minehead at the planning stage of the monorail in 1967 when he instructed managers to walk with him as he paced out the 800-yard route. Each manager carried with him a pole with a plant pot on top. When Billy stopped, the manager was instructed to plant the pole, which was to be the marker for the support stanchions of the monorail; thus Billy actually personally created the design for this particular monorail. The last train ran in 1996.

The Minehead camp was opened on 26 May 1962, after an investment of £2 million. The site was chosen after Billy allegedly had an aerial search conducted in South West England. Once the campers had arrived some were to form a committee to help with various activities and to assist with competitions.

The Minehead Centre, situated near Exmoor and the Bristol Channel, seemed to take on the mantle of an outdoor pursuit area, as demonstrated by the number of activities available. It covered over 165 acres of former grazing marshes. A large boating lake was constructed, when the soil was removed to make a barrier to prevent flooding. Part of the boating lake was filled in during 1992 to make way for a new fun fair.

The crazy golf area never fails to entertain, pitting parents against children. It is very often the area of most noise, with excitement rising as groups head for the winning post.

BUTLIN'S MINEHEAD
Panorama from Ski Slope

The dry ski slope was opened in the 1960s and removed in 1970. Here we see a camper receiving expert instruction from Redcoat Doug MacLeod, newly arrived from Aviemore in Scotland. Doug spent many years with the company, eventually becoming entertainment manager then general manager at Minehead.

Waterskiing was available at Minehead in the 1960s with instruction and demonstrations provided daily. Dave Simpson, seen in the speedboat, and Garth Thomas, instructor, were part of a six-man team which included Roger Billington, the current Butlin's archivist. Their own instruction came from a trip to a local library to read up on the subject.

Amusement parks were where the story started for Billy and therefore it was natural that they should also appear on his holiday camps. Some sites had more than others and this view shows some of the earlier rides that guests could enjoy. This outdoor venue was moved in 1992 alongside major changes on the camp.

At Minehead, two years after the camp opened, Bobbie Butlin (second left) and Paul Winterforde-Young from Executive Social Services (second from the right) take a well earned rest in the Amusement Park whilst showing Reginald Maudlin, Conservative MP, and his wife around the camp.

Do you remember the revolving carousel bars, which were set up in the larger bars on all centres in the early 1960s? There was usually a popular band playing and guests would return nightly.

Numerous miniature trains operated throughout the company and the engines were often swapped between camps. As some camps were larger than others, the route could be either a straight A to B or a more circular one. Over the years at Minehead it operated at three different locations. These trains operated at various times between 1956 and 1996.

In the 1980s Minehead was lucky enough to receive a visit from five Disney characters, much to the delight of the holidaymakers.

Each year Billy would fill Earls Court Olympia with his rides and attractions. It was at Olympia in the late 1920s that he was first shown drawings of the American dodgems. He was so interested that he spent £2,000 buying a car. Here at Minehead, fifty years later, they continued to provide the thrills first encouraged by Billy in the 1930s.

Barry Island was the last and smallest camp to be built and opened on 18 June 1966. Occupying just 45 acres on the peninsular known as Neil's Point, this hilly area required Butlin's to build three-tiered chalet lines with several steps and stairs needed for access between buildings. In 1967 a chairlift was also opened to help ease the the climb!

Upon entering the camp, this three-storey building seen beyond the outdoor swimming pools, was to accommodate Butlin's attractions, which included the Repertory Theatre, Whist Lounge, Licensed Bar, Coffee Bar and the Indoor Swimming Pool. The *Puffing Billy* train in the foreground was kept busy transporting everyone around. Sadly, the camp's lifespan under the Butlin banner was only twenty years and it closed on 31 December 1986. It was sold to Majestic Holidays and was operated by them for a further ten years. The Council eventually bought the centre and demolished part of it on which to build 250 homes.

Outdoor swimming pools became less popular and were transformed into themed outdoor fun pools for children, giving them a new lease of life. Only part of the Barry Island large tiered outdoor pool was adapted into a children's fun pool.

With special facilities for children available, families took advantage of the group events organised by the Junior Leaders Redcoats at each centre. The sound of children laughing and enjoying themselves would ring out across the camps to the amusement of their parents, who were engaged in their own activities. 'Happy children means happy parents means happy holidays' was a slogan used at one time on a Butlin's carnival float.

At the early centres meals were served four times a day, but the pattern eventually transferred into three meals a day in two sittings. However, when you consider that the small camps had 5,000 guests and the larger 12,000 per week, you can appreciate the numbers that were accommodated at each sitting per meal. In 1961 it was thought that twenty-one million cups of tea were drunk, 700,000 loaves of bread eaten and five and a half million eggs enjoyed.

The waiters and waitresses in the dining halls had a very difficult job. Dining halls could accommodate up to 2,000 guests per sitting, all wanting their meals quickly and hot. Many local people recall working in the dining halls while they were students during their summer vacation. Due to the length of the summer season, thousands of youngsters applied to the company for vocational work. The company even flew in staff from places like Iceland and Hungary to work for a set number of weeks. This photograph was taken at Barry Island.

Above Competitions were the hallmark of the company for a number of years, some of which were taken from popular television programmes of the time. Above we see guests at Barry Island taking part in an *It's a Knockout*-style event.

Left A necessary service provided at the camps were the medical departments. Each medical department would be staffed by fully qualified SRN's (State Registered Nurses) and a local doctor would take a surgery each morning for the benefit of guests and staff. If there was a medical emergency anywhere on a centre, a nurse would be despatched to deal with the problem. These staff could be involved with any eventuality from a birth to a death.

three

Hotels

In the late 1940s, as the six holiday camps in Britain were established, other avenues were explored to extend the Butlin's empire. A holiday in the Bahamas gave Billy the idea to build there specifically to attract the American market. In 1948 he began construction of a 'vacation village' on the island of Grand Bahamas, which would be staffed entirely with English personnel. The 500 labourers employed on the construction were provided with basic accommodation and a cinema. In addition, he offered to build an airport with direct flights to the island. The vacation village eventually opened in January 1950, unfortunately coinciding with the Korean War (1950-53), which adversely affected the American economy. The first six months saw only 17,000 visitors, far less than anticipated, and Billy had to accept that Americans were not attracted to this holiday concept.

With the loss of support from some of his financial backers, the devaluation of the pound due to the war, and unsustainable costs, Billy was forced to accept that the project had failed, which was all the more disappointing as he had invested a large amount of his own personal fortune.

Back in Britain in 1950, as holidaymakers began seeking holidays outside the normal May to September season, he was prompted to diversify into the hotel trade. Rather than build new hotels, he chose to acquire existing hotels in primary seaside resorts. They were refurbished, a holiday entertainment package based on the format at the camps was introduced, and Redcoats who had stage experience were employed. The initial group of hotels was opened in Brighton, Margate and Blackpool between 1953 and 1956, and a further four at Scarborough, Torremolinos (Spain), Llandudno and London between 1978 and 1979. It was not long before Billy had another success on his hands with the provision of all-year-round hotel holidays in addition to the southern camps at Bognor, Clacton and Minehead, which had been open for winter weekends since the early 1960s.

In the early 1970s (later than other holiday camp operators), Butlin's decided to increase the self-catering operation and so set up a Small Centres Division. This consisted of a number of small holiday camps, caravan and camping parks and later boatyards, which were acquired between 1971 and 1981. Initially many were in Cornwall and in 1976 these smaller outlets were marketed under the title of Freshfields.

With holidays abroad becoming increasingly popular, the number of visitors to holiday camps and hotels in the UK during the late 1960s started to decline. A decade later, when Butlin's was owned by the Rank Organisation, some of the camps and hotels were closed and sold off. For similar reasons, the Freshfields sites were eventually sold.

The following pages show that some of the hotels are still operating, but others have long since been demolished or converted into apartments. However, memories of Butlin's holidays are still vivid to those guests who frequently visited the hotels. Many will remember young Redcoats who welcomed the opportunity to improve their stage act – Redcoats like the late Ted Rogers, Dave Allen, Jimmy Tarbuck, Freddie 'Parrot Face' Davies and Johnny Ball, to name but a few.

Billy's first attempt at seeking pastures new came after he took a vacation in the Bahamas in 1946. Liking the area, he recognised the future potential and purchased two hotels, one of which was the Fort Montague Beach in Nassau. He then set about renovating it, in a British style to appeal to the wealthy American market.

In 1948 Billy formed Butlin's (Bahamas) Ltd to enable him to build a 'vacation village', which he partially opened the following year. Hoping to attract middle-class Americans and Canadians, he designed the village with an 'olde worlde' English theme and staffed it almost entirely with English workers. For the vacation village he even instituted his own coins, which had the Queen's head on one side and animals on the other. By the 1960s some of these coins had been sunk into the floor of a bar for decoration. Unfortunately, due to construction and labour problems (an airport needed to be built) and the Korean War, overseas investment dried up and the village's fate was sealed. Billy himself lost in the region of £4 million (at today's prices) with this venture.

BUTLIN'S OCEAN HOTEL, SALTDEAN, BRIGHTON

The first Butlin's hotel was the art-deco Ocean Hotel at Saltdean, Brighton, which was built in 1938. Billy acquired it for £250,000 and opened it on 2 May 1953. He wanted to branch into hotels as the camps were limited to the summer season. His opening advertisement stated: 'It offers virtually the same amenities as a Butlin Camp plus the thrill of a "land cruise" and the comfort of an up-to-the-minute self-contained hotel.'

This group of guests posed for a souvenir photograph to provide the perfect memory of their holiday. The Ocean Hotel has a special place in the memory of many guests and staff, so much so that during 2009 and 2010, during redevelopment of the hotel into luxury apartments, many visited to see the progress. The main art-deco hotel was converted but all other buildings were demolished and rebuilt. When the authors visited in 2009 they were told by the sales team that several ex-guests had shown interest in buying apartments.

THE RECEPTION HALL.   BUTLIN'S OCEAN HOTEL, SALTDEAN, BRIGHTON. B.150

Redcoats were in attendance in the reception hall on intake days (day of arrival) to assist and advise guests. They also ran sports activities and competitions as well as entertaining the guests. It was whilst Dave Allen was working as a Redcoat at the Ocean Hotel that he was spotted by a talent scout and had his first break on television.

THE BALLROOM.   BUTLIN'S OCEAN HOTEL, SALTDEAN, BRIGHTON.   B.155

The art-deco theme was echoed in the ballroom. These ballrooms housed dance lessons in the mornings, practice in the afternoon and sequined dresses and evening suits in the evening. The hotel was sold in 1999 to the Grand Hotel Group and remained open until 2005. The main building is Grade II listed and has since been converted into apartments.

'Sunbather's paradise' was how Billy advertised this feature of his new Ocean Hotel. The glass-protected sun decks became the guests' favourite place to relax in the sun, or simply enjoy the view across the English Channel.

This photograph was taken in 2009 on a visit made to see the changes to the ex-Ocean Hotel at Saltdean. Sylvia, who worked here for a few months in 1976, was pleased to see the outward appearance of this building had been retained. The hotel has been transformed into luxury flats and apartments, whilst retaining some of the interior grandeur of the original art-deco hotel.

Originally built in 1776, this hotel has a chequered history, being renamed the Metropole in 1896. Billy acquired it with a long lease in 1955. Having become run down during the Second World War, when it was used by the RAF, it had very little business. Billy began offering evening entertainment and holiday packages, and bookings soon increased. He immediately added a conservatory bar and café and had to turn the garden into a car park due to demand. The Metropole Hotel holds a unique site on Blackpool's seafront, being the only hotel built on the seaward side of the promenade.

Mable Worrall was the manageress of the Metropole and became synonymous with any mention of its name throughout the company and Blackpool. When Billy bought the hotel she had already been working there for two years. She said she couldn't be happier than working there and only the best was good enough for her hotel, and she fought to keep standards high. Some of her staff stayed with her for over twenty years. She was known as the 'Walking Encyclopaedia' and on her retirement she remained and stayed in her usual accommodation within the hotel.

These four hotels were bought by Billy in 1955. Clockwise from top left: St George's, Queens Hotel, Norfolk Hotel, Florence Hotel. They were situated overlooking spacious lawns and gardens leading down to the beach and Cliftonville seafront, with the resort of Margate nearby.

The following year, 1956, Billy bought the Grand (right), adjacent to the Norfolk and St Georges (seen in the distance), which he marketed as the Cliftonville Hotels. While guests were booked into a particular hotel they were free to enjoy the facilities of all. In the 1990s an underground walkway was created to join the three hotels to enable guests to move around in the dry and warm. They were sold in 1999 and resold in 2004. Both the Grand and the Norfolk were then demolished the following year.

The large Queen's Hotel was situated in close proximity to the sea and was separated from the other three hotels by gardens with large lawns in between. A large indoor swimming pool was the main feature of this hotel. It was here that Billy first saw an indoor pool with glass windows in the sides, an idea he was to introduce into all his holiday camps. Eventually this pool was transformed into a dolphinarium. The Queen's Hotel was closed and demolished in the late 1970s.

BUTLIN'S ST. GEORGE'S HOTEL, CLIFTONVILLE   L 927

St George's Hotel was the most intimate of all the hotels and remained open after the demolition of the other two. The Ship Bar was open to non-residents and proved very popular with the locals. There was also a Cave Bar in the basement, which was a spit and sawdust venue. This hotel finally closed and was demolished in 2007/8.

The dining room in the hotels were arranged in a similar style to the main holiday camps. At some hotels a photographer was contracted to take pictures at breakfast so that they could produce the memorable red keyrings for sale at the evening meal. In the early years the photographs were in black and white, but in the 1960s a novelty keyring viewer was introduced. The photographs were taken on colour transparency and these were inserted into the viewer and could be seen by simply holding it to the eye. No doubt some readers may still have one.

BUTLIN'S GRAND HOTEL
Cliftonville, Margate

The Grand Hotel was originally called the Cliftonville Hydro and still had tiling in the basement from the Hydro days when bought by Billy in 1956, which was also the year he began offering special weekend packages. In the 1990s the accommodation consisted of 268 bedrooms including a fully equipped self-catering apartment with two bedrooms and sitting room.

Billy was always the first to catch on to the latest trend or craze. The Espresso Coffee Bar soon became a popular venue for younger guests, as seen here at the Norfolk Hotel in 1966.

The Grand Hotel at Scarborough was built in 1867 and is a very impressive building, dominating its surroundings from its site on St Nicholas Cliff overlooking South Bay. A cliffside lift, beside the hotel, takes guest to the beachside promenade. It was once Europe's premier hotel but when bought by Billy in 1978 it had falling guest numbers and was vulnerable to conversion into holiday flats. Billy, however, had plans for refurbishment and with the introduction of his well-known holiday package the hotel was soon attracting new clientele.

Inside the main entrance you came into the hall and there before you was a magnificent staircase which rose to the upper floors, and was surrounded by a series of tall, stately arches, which lead up to the domed ceiling. It is stated that the architect of the hotel, Cuthbert Broderick, built the staircase wide enough to allow two ladies in crinolines and their partners to easily pass each other.

Left Butlin's entered the foreign package holiday market in 1979, acquiring the modern three-star, 414-room hotel El Griego in Torremolinos on the Costa Del Sol, Spain. It was eventually sold but the hotel is still open today, renamed Hotel Griego Mar.

Below There was an indoor and outdoor swimming pool at the El Griego. One of the brochures stated that 'your relaxing holiday in the sun starts from the moment the Redcoats welcome you at Malaga airport and escort you to the hotel.'

The Grand Hotel at Llandudno, North Wales was purchased in 1981. It was an excellent addition to the company with stunning scenery and old-world charm which couldn't be bettered. It was situated right on the seafront, with the majestic headlands of the Great Orme and Little Orme on either side and the peaks of Snowdonia in the background. Horse-drawn carriage rides could be taken along the prom to the pier. In 1998 this hotel was sold to a private company.

When, in 1994, the company bought the Grand Hotel in Bayswater London, it was a major boost for Butlin's holidaymakers. They could take full advantage of the Butlin's package-prices and entertainment on the doorstep of what London had to offer. In the company's usual style, a free daily Red Bus Tour was arranged, with a Redcoat tour guide. The hotel also had its own theatre ticket agency to assist you to book the top London shows. It was only five years later, in 1999, that the company sadly made the decision to sell all their hotels.

Under the banner of Small Centres, the company's second purchase in 1972 was
Duporth, St Austell, Cornwall. The Manor House was demolished in 1979 amid
stories of ghosts regularly appearing to guests. Eventually this site was sold.

Billy had numerous amusement parks, one of which was situated on the seafront at Hayling Island.
Years later he was to purchase the Sunshine Holiday Camp, whose capacity was under 1,000, also on
Hayling Island. This was reached after driving along a small country lane, culminating in this view
across Chichester Harbour in West Sussex.

four

The Nursery Department

One of the most important aspects of any holiday is the care of children. Billy recognised this and quickly provided a nursery service on each of his holiday camps. As early as 1946, when Clacton was due to reopen after the Second World War, Billy employed Anne Hayter to organise childcare for two to five-year-olds. Encouraged by what Anne accomplished, he asked that she extend this service to all centres. Anne put forward a comprehensive plan for a nursery service that became an important attraction for family holidays and of course it gave Butlin's another key feature to advertise.

By the 1950s a full nursery service was in operation at all camps, catering for children from nought to two years. This format ran for many years, on the lines of a day nursery with additional facilities offered. The service was an innovation and revelation as most parents had no access to a nursery service. The Butlin's nursery offered bottle preparation, an infant feeding centre providing well-known brands of baby food, play rooms, pushchair hire, and even a nappy washing service, as in those early years there were no disposable nappies. A nursery laundress would wash in excess of 300 nappies daily, returning them the following morning washed and aired.

Another service appreciated by parents was the evening chalet patrol. Nurses patrolled the chalet lines listening for distressed babies whilst their parents enjoyed the entertainment in the knowledge that their children were safe. In the 1980s the security department took over the chalet patrol service.

Anne Hayter eventually retired in the early 1970s and her role as head of nurseries was transferred to Butlin's executive, Paul Winterforde-Young. A senior nursery matron, Rosina Hosking, was appointed to oversee the operation. After four years in this capacity, Rosina Hosking retired and was succeeded by Shirley Lewis (co-author of this book), who held the position for sixteen years using Paul Winterforde-Young's philosophy 'the best possible service, always with a smile.'

In 1986 Paul Winterforde-Young retired and was succeeded by Butlin executive Gerry Cable. This change coincided with the permanent closures of the camps at Filey and Clacton. Gerry Cable set out to bring the nursery buildings up to date and created a theme at each; Minehead was redesigned to replicate a castle, Skegness had a nursery rhyme theme, and all other sites were similarly upgraded. In 1988 a new, smaller nursery was built at Bognor Regis and main catering took over the feeding of infants. The original infant dining rooms became 'Rumpus Rooms', where parents could stay and play with their children.

The staff at any one nursery included a matron, deputy matron, senior nurses, nursery nurse trained (NNEB), a cook, a domestic, a laundress and a handyman. During the 1970s, there were major changes in the service, which saw the handyman role moved to the accommodation department. Likewise with the introduction of disposable nappies, the laundress services were no longer required. Originally the summer season lasted for a period of eighteen to twenty weeks, increasing to twenty-six weeks with the addition of new southern-based camps. In later years all-year-round holidays saw the introduction of permanent staff. Through the 1960s, each nursery would employ approximately thirty-five staff but by the 1980s it was more a care and play service where only ten or twelve staff were required.

Butlin's nursery staff were aware that a well cared-for child ensured a good holiday for all the family and always strived to give the best possible care. As Billy always said, 'Listen to the guests and action their wishes.'

Prior to every season, nursery matrons were invited to attend a pre-season conference. Pictured are matrons meeting at Bognor Regis in 1962. From left to right: -?- (secretary to Mrs Hayter), Beryl Rigby (Filey), Janine Benson (Clacton), Rosina Hopkins (Pwllheli), Mildred Wright (Bognor), Mary Wall (Skegness), Joyce Crawford (Skegness deputy), -?- (Minehead), and Mrs Anne Hayter, who initiated the nursery service for Butlin's. Following Anne's retirement, her role as head of nurseries passed to Rosina Hoskins.

Famous people were not averse to visiting the nursery department for a photo opportunity and here we see Godfrey Winn in the nursery outdoor play area in Bognor Regis in the 1960s. For security reasons, all children aged five years and under were given a tie-on name tag before being left in the nursery. Ultimately, the company adopted the use of identity bracelets, an item in general use in the twenty-first century.

In the early 1960s, the Filey nursery bore the 'showman' influence with a large roundabout and an electric galleon. There were numerous rocking horses and Mobo horses on which children could ride, plus soft toys, building bricks and books. Some children took a while to settle into the nursery and it was with a feeling of great satisfaction that nurses could say goodbye to a happy, smiling child at the end of the week.

Opposite Children under the age of two were fed by their parents in the Infants' Feeding Centre. After the meal they would be left to sleep in a cot or play with the nursery nurses in the huge playpens. Parents were then able to go to the main dining room to enjoy their own meal. Mealtimes in the nursery were very busy as there could be up to seventy hungry children to feed at a time.

The playrooms were constantly being adapted to keep the children happy and amused. Joan Stonely, Minehead Nursery Matron, is seen here on the right in 1973 visiting the shop the nursery nurses themselves had set up and stocked. Later, separate messy arts and crafts areas were created and a television/book room was built within the nursery.

Nursery nurses in fancy dress on Christmas Day at Bognor Regis, 1988. They enjoyed helping Santa Claus to distribute presents to the young children in the theatre, prior to giving them a special day of fun in the nursery. With the advent of Winter Weekend Opening, a percentage of nursery and other department employees became permanent staff, so besides running the guests' nursery it was necessary to open a staff crèche for two to five year olds for local employees.

The Skegness nursery kitchen and servery, pictured here in the mid-1960s, was an open-plan design and linked to the dining area. This allowed parents to see their child's food preparation. Each nursery had its own cook who prepared an excellent variety of food from which parents could choose and which would be served to the children by the nurses.

The Infants' Feeding Centre at Mosney in the 1970s. It was quite a sight to see up to eighty babies being fed in long lines of highchairs all at one time. Low tables and chairs were an alternative for parents' use.

BUTLIN'S CHILD CRYING SERVIC
Please contact us at:—
THE BEACHCOMBER BAR
OR
PRINCES BUILDINGS.
From....7.30........p.m. to....8.30....p.m.
From....8.30........p.m. to....11.11....p.m.

Above To allow guests to enjoy their evening entertainment, a chalet patrol service operated between 5.30 p.m. and 11.30 p.m. Parents would register their child and chalet number with the nurses and list the entertainment venues they intended to visit during the evening. Children could be put safely to bed and once asleep they were assured of regular visits to the chalet by the patrolling nurses. On finding a child crying, a 'Baby Crying' message was sent to the appropriate venue to alert the parents. This service was discontinued in the 1990s when Government legislation stated that children should not be left unattended. Butlin's then introduced a babysitting service.

Left The nursery staff love having a reason to give the children a party and a chance to dress up. The wedding of Prince Charles and Princess Diana in 1981 was a great excuse for the children and staff at Bognor Regis to enjoy themselves. The adults, from left to right, are: Mary Woodward (senior nurse), –?–, Freda Luck (nursery matron), Pamela ?, –?–, –?–, –?–.

Ann Brandon, nursery matron at Ayr, with two of her staff in 1963 wearing the easily recognisable uniform of the nursery nurses. This hospital-style uniform, with belts, caps and cloaks, was adopted for forty years. In 1988, times were changing and camps were allowed to choose their own uniforms. By 1996 further changes saw the introduction of a modern polo shirt and trousers. Ann Brandon was one of a number of nursery staff who began work as a young nursery nurse, then married, had her own family and later returned as nursery matron.

After entertaining the children, Rod Hull and Emu posed with nursery nurses in the Rumpus Room at Minehead. The nurses had made their own colourful tabards appliquéd with motifs such as butterflies, flowers, balloons and kites. The idea stemmed from an outfit worn by Boy George when he sang 'Karma Chameleon'.

Forty members of the nursery staff in their annual group photograph at Minehead in 1974. Joining the group were, Shirley Lewis (operations manager, seated centre in the second row), Joan Stonely (nursery matron), Tony Crosby (general manager), Paul Winterforde-Young (executive social services), Diana Wall (PA to Paul Winterforde-Young).

By 1994 the nurseries were more involved with 'play', which called for small staff numbers. Hence the smaller annual group photograph for Bognor Regis in that year. From left to right, back row: Emma Kennerley, Karen Holland, Simon Mitchell, Dawn Ambrose, Jo Davies. Middle row: Karen Tucker, Emma Lloyd, Wendy Kimber, Sally Carder, Kerrie Doke, Nichola Spain. Front row: Nikki Broom, Angela Davies (deputy manager), Jill Conway (crèche supervisor), Paul Selby (entertainments manager), Shirley Lewis (nursery manager), Paula Stubbs, Miriam McElroy.

five

Entertainment

The first Redcoat was born when Billy Butlin asked one of his assistants, Norman Bradford, to use a microphone to encourage campers to participate in planned activities. So successful was he that he was instructed to wear a red jacket to ensure he stood out in the crowd. This was also the time when the inimitable slogan Hi-De-Hi was born.

Something for everyone was the theme. Campers could choose to sit back and relax or join in the numerous activities available to them. Thousands willingly took part in the various competitions which included the famous Knobbly Knees, Bonny Babies, Glamorous Grandmothers and Holiday Princess, to mention but a few. Billy Butlin knew that he had found something very special when he witnessed the enjoyment on campers' faces.

Entertainment was the hallmark of every Butlin camp with well-known names from the entertainment business, sport and the silver screen appearing alongside resident entertainers engaged for the summer season. With the opening of more and more camps, the professional entertainment became even more sophisticated, with each site having its own resident Revue Company – a complete package of acts, scenery, dancers and music. Each show covered a two-week period to ensure that campers taking a fortnight's holiday would enjoy different performances during their second week.

The numerous attractions included a Sunday Variety Show with visiting artistes, a Lucky Dip Show (which invited audience participation with the opportunity to win prizes), the Campers' Talent Show (which culminated in a Grand Final held on many occasions at the London Palladium), and, of course, the ever popular Redcoat Show. To satisfy those campers who wished to enjoy something more serious, each camp had a resident Repertory Company, performing three plays a week in their own theatrical venue. In addition to all this, there were regular feature film shows with a different film each night. Children were always a priority at each Butlin camp and they could enjoy their own cartoon films which preceded a show by the professional children's entertainer.

Dancing to live bands was always popular and campers could choose from three large ballrooms which catered for modern dance, old time and sequence dancing and, in the late 1950s, rock'n'roll was introduced. No expense was spared in providing first-class bands.

One of Billy Butlin's mottos was 'No publicity is bad publicity' and he encouraged his visitors to recommend his holidays to their friends and family. In later years, when the Butlin name was associated with numerous sponsored events, he always ensured that there were professionally printed programmes. These souvenir programmes covered all the popular Butlin's sponsored events, such as darts tournaments, show jumping, ladies' team gymnastics, cross Channel swimming race, pony club mounted games, players' circuit snooker, Donald Campbell's *Bluebird* water speed attempts, John O'Groats to Land's End walking race and the Duke of Edinburgh Award Scheme, to mention but a few. Entrance to all these theatre shows was free of charge to campers, the only exception being the Late Night Cabaret, which featured top professional artists and which commenced in the early 1970s. Those campers not wishing to participate in any of the entertainment on offer could relax in one of the comfortable lounges, and simply enjoy the beautiful scenery that surrounded the camp.

This 1955 entertainment programme promotes some of the wide range of events and activities available for guests to enjoy.

Opposite above Every year the entertainment department had a mid-season group photograph taken and copies of most of these are still safely kept in the archives. On the camps, many copies were sold as souvenirs to holidaymakers. This group picture was taken in 1957 at Pwllheli.

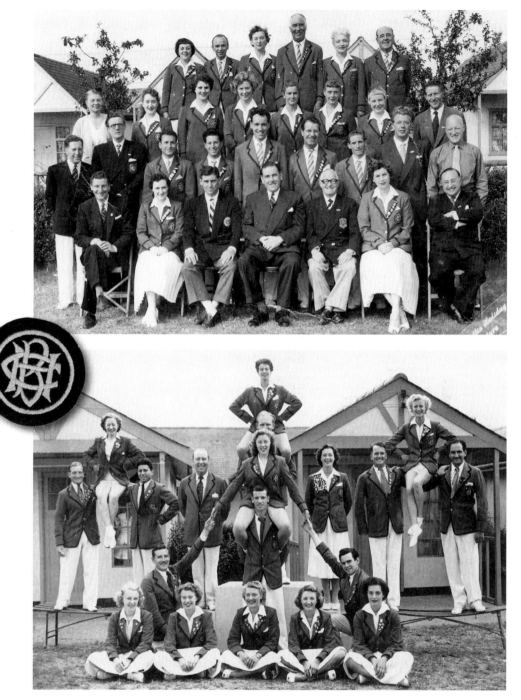

The familiar Redcoat uniform was not always what it seemed – in the early days staff only received the red jacket and had to purchase the rest of the uniform themselves. But in 1957 this changed and white shirts/blouses, white flannels/pleated skirts and plastic raincoats were issued too. The early jackets had a black braid around the lapels and cuffs; in 1957 this braid changed to royal blue and in the 1970s the braid was removed. In 1988, fashion icon Zandra Rhodes was called in to revamp the whole uniform.

In 1960 Richard Starkey received an offer of a thirteen-week summer engagement at Butlin's in Pwllheli, which at first he turned down, but eventually carried out. In 1962 he was transferred to Skegness. He was engaged as drummer with rock band Rory Storm and the Hurricanes. He eventually changed his named to Ringo Starr and was working at Butlin's when he received a call to join a new band called The Beatles, with John Lennon and Paul McCartney.

The popular Horse of the Year Show events were held on six camps with three heats in one day; Novice, Championship and Top Score, the latter two being qualifiers for the Horse of the Year Show at Wembley Arena. First, second and third would go forward. The first night at Wembley, from 1963 to 1982, was known as Butlin's Night and the stadium was a colourful sight with Redcoats acting as ushers. Here we see Diana Dors, Bobbie Butlin, David Broome (rider) and Eamonn Andrews, who at the time was Director of Entertainments for Butlins and was visiting Pwllheli in 1973.

Brenda Cresswell (*née* Maguire) is seen here ready to make announcements and play records for Radio Butlin. The service started in 1946 and continued until the late 1970s. The various calls to meals, events and competitions were all part of the great chemistry of the holiday centres. It was often described as the nerve centre of the camps, which encouraged campers to join in the fun that was available for all to enjoy. Radio Butlin operated from early morning to 11.15 p.m., seven days a week.

Over the years there were many competitions 'sponsored' by prominent organisations. Seen here at the Brighton Hotel are the successful semi-finalists of the 1979 Southern Region 'Miss She' event, a day-wear competition which was also judged upon charm, personality and grooming. Ladies aged between eighteen and eighty years of age could enter the 'Miss She', which became the longest sponsored event ever held at Butlin's. This popular magazine sponsored this weekly competition from 1955 to 1983 and at one time there were over 10,000 entries in a year. The winner of the 1964 competition, Miss Ann Sidney, went on to become Miss World.

Dancing in all its forms has been a popular activity throughout the Butlin's organisation. This programme was for a 1948 event in Earls Court. Dance styles have changed over the years but the company has always embraced the changing styles. Sylvia remembers watching the men in bow ties and evening suits and the ladies in their sequined dresses, old time dancing over the Christmas period in Bognor Regis.

Right Back in 1940, Butlin's held the Butlin's Professional Dance Championship at the Royal Opera House Covent Garden, organised by Captain J. Russell Pickering. In 1948, the first National Veleta Competition was run by Teddy Ryan. He was succeeded by Wilfred Orange until his mantle was taken over by Roger Billington.

Below The trophy winners at the 1957 Filey Dance Festival. Butlin's presented some of the world's largest music and dance festivals with over 60,000 participants per annum. The variety of styles included ballroom, highland, stage, disco, folk, country and western and many more. The Carl–Alan Award was presented to Sir William Butlin MBE, Wilfred Orange and Roger Billington for their services to dance.

Billy met Marlene Dietrich in 1955 and was amazed that a lady so glamorous could also be a grandmother. Thus the 'Glamorous Grandmother' competition was born, with each weekly winner being invited to a semi-final either in the north or south, depending on their home address. From these semi-finals, ten from each went through to the Grand Final. Pictured here is Susan Brown, winner of the 1985 competition, with judges David Jacobs, Alison Holloway, Bill Roach, Ted Rogers and Gloria Hunniford.

The Glamorous Grandmother competition became the biggest competition ever run by Butlin's, it attracted a great deal of publicity and companies were keen to sponsor it. At its height there could be 10,000 entries per year, with ladies returning year after year. Here we see the ten successful ladies – posing with the five judges – from the Southern Area semi-final who will go through to the Grand Final later in the year. The competition ran from 1955 until 1997, when Butlin's felt that it had become 'time expired'.

Taken at Clacton in 1957, we see the 'Vocaltones', who eventually changed their name to the 'Butlinaires' after they were contracted to tour a number of camps. Their singing style was a four-part harmony in the style of a Welsh male-voice choir. Note the pocket handkerchiefs, worn according to which side of the microphone they stood. The picture shows the five 'Vocaltones' with two other talent show winners.

Right Many famous people began their careers at Butlin's. The young Beverley Sisters entertained here and a twelve-year-old Julie Andrews performed with her parents. In 1979 a young girl called Catherine was a finalist in the Junior Star Trail. Over the years she appeared on television until eventually she went to America and became known to the world as Catherine Zeta Jones CBE, the film star wife of Michael Douglas.

Hughie Green visited Butlin's holiday camps before the war, when, in addition to entertaining on stage, he spent a great deal of time with the campers. It was Hughie who, in the late 1960s, was booked for late night cabarets on a trial run to see if they would be popular. A big name at the time always topped the bill and these shows quickly became hugely popular.

Jon Pertwee giving out autographs in the 1960s. According to a 1961 programme, the 'Road to Fame' was the 'Butlin Way'. Today people appear on television talent shows and then go to Butlin's to entertain the guests, thus Butlin's are still continuing to provide a platform for entertainers.

Each centre had their own children's entertainer called 'Uncle' and a children's theatre. Here we see ventriloquist Uncle Boko at Skegness in 1948 entertaining children with his dummy. He began at Skegness after the Second World War and became a much loved and well-known figure in his red fez. He entertained many generations of children, still working at Skegness until his death in 1960. Another of his duties was to be Master of Ceremonies for all the children's competitions.

Butlin **BEAVER CLUB RULES**

1. **B** e kind to dumb animals.

2. **E** ager always to help others.

3. **A** im to be clean, neat and tidy.

4. **V** ictory by Fair Play.

5. **E** nergetic at work and play.

6. **R** espect for parents and all elders.

and in all things

BE AS EAGER AS A BEAVER

A club for six to eleven year olds was thought up by Frank Mansell, who came up with the name 'Butlin Beavers Club'. Anne Hayter worked with Frank to set up the club in 1951/2. Redcoats would encourage children to join at the beginning of their holiday. They received a membership card, a badge and met at their specially-constructed Beaver Lodge for meetings. Billy ensured that every Beaver received a birthday card, a Christmas card and a present. A Butlin Beaver annual was produced every year. By 1962 there were over 200,000 Beavers nationwide. The Beaver Club continued into the 1980s.

There were snooker rooms at all centres, with up to 100 tables at the larger camps. John Pulman, former snooker World Champion, would provide demonstrations as he toured Butlin's for the duration of the season, promoting the *Daily Mail* sponsorship of the weekly snooker tournament.

To increase Butlin's publicity, the company sponsored the Grand Masters Darts Tournament, which was held in Birmingham and featured on Central Television for ten years. The contestants were all professional darts players.

One of Butlin's Luxury Holiday Camp Ballrooms

During the 1950s and '60s over five million people went dancing weekly and Billy picked up on the trend by providing at least three ballrooms at each holiday camp and two in hotels. According to a 1960s camp programme, 'almost every dance band in the country played at Butlin's'. Names included Ivy Benson, Mantovani, Harry Roy and many more. It was anticipated that there would be around 700 musicians playing during the summer season. Their music covered all the popular dance crazes of the time. There was dancing instruction in old time and sequence six days a week.

One of the musicians was Eric Winstone, who became the resident band leader at Clacton after the war. He stayed with the company, playing at various sites until the late 1950s. He was a successful composer and his signature tune, 'Stage Coach', was popular. During the winter months he was known as 'Uncle Eric' on Radio Luxembourg in a special programme for members of the Butlin Beaver Club. Eventually the stagecoach shape was used for yet another badge. The Stagecoach once stood on a playing field near the seashore at Clacton before being moved to the Crazy Horse Saloon as part of the décor.

Crowds of people enjoying themselves is one of the prevailing memories for all who have ever visited Butlin's. Ed Stewart made periodic visits to Pwllheli for his Radio 1 show, as here in 1982. Many outside organisations would use the Butlin centres for major events, mainly due to the number of people who were readily available to become involved or simply watch and enjoy the events.

Redcoats were involved with leading guests to events or activities. Following the Sunday morning get-together the holidaymakers would line up behind their respective house banners, of which there could be as many as six, marching behind the band to one of the large licensed bars, where a lunchtime concert would be held. Here we see Brian Freeman (on the left) and Ron Stanway (on the right) holding the Edinburgh House banner. Ron joined the company in 1954 as a Redcoat and eventually retired in 1988 as General Manager for Entertainments and Promotions.

SIX

... And The Rest

The name Butlin's is synonymous with holiday camps and hotels but, in delving into the history of the company, it was surprising how many other activities, promotions and sponsorships carried the Butlin name, hence the title of this chapter '... And the rest'.

Billy's original concept for holidaymakers provided all the basic requirements enjoyed at home. In addition to the entertainment venues, outlets such as 'Mollie Rowntree' hairdressing salons for ladies and gentlemen were introduced at all camps, alongside shops and even post offices, which provided all the usual services.

In 1946, with so many campers visiting, Billy recognised the need for worship and with the full co-operation of the Church of England, made provision for a chapel on every camp. Some camps also had a Roman Catholic church. Over the years, numerous religious organisations had exclusive use of the camps for their annual conventions.

Following the 'Beeching' cutbacks of the railways in the 1960s, famous old steam engines were bought by Billy, refurbished and sited on the camps as yet another attraction. As the number of camps increased, transportation became paramount to enable Billy to travel quickly. He purchased small aircraft, painting some of them his distinctive yellow and blue, with his 'B' emblazoned on the side, landing at airstrips close to the camps from where a Butlin concessionaire provided daily pleasure flights.

Souvenirs were extremely popular and the shops displayed a variety of items which included mugs, leather wallets, key cases and coins, to name just a few, some of which are now collectors' items. The major souvenir from Butlin's was, and still is, the Butlin Badge, issued at all camps from 1936 until 1967. However, in recent years the company have produced badges that can be purchased by guests and collectors.

Many holidaymakers benefited from coaching in popular sports like football, cricket, table tennis, snooker, darts and fencing. Parties taking part in the Duke of Edinburgh's Award Scheme were invited to Ayr, Filey, Minehead or Pwllheli where the surrounding countryside was most suitable. In later years, School Venture Weeks also provided a wide range of educational skills for thousands of young people, and included cycling proficiency classes.

Millions of holidaymakers have visited Butlin's, but it was also the place to be seen by famous people from all walks of life. These included stars of film, stage, radio and television, many of whom visited for a day, together with various sport stars participating in coaching or making a personal appearance. The ultimate accolade was a visit to Pwllheli in 1963 by Her Majesty the Queen and Prince Philip, not forgetting a visit to Ayr in the 1960s by Dwight D. Eisenhower, the then President of the United States.

Various events formed an integral part of the history of Butlin's and Sir William Butlin MBE took every opportunity to obtain advertising, with such events as the John O'Groats to Land's End walking race, swimming races across the English Channel, show jumping; the list is endless. His biggest disappointment was not being able to display the Butlin logo in red neon lighting above the revolving Top of the Tower restaurant in London, which he and his son Bobbie had acquired. It was considered to be a danger to aircraft approaching Heathrow.

The authors have attempted to capture the flavour of 'Butlin's', and it is hoped that this book will have awakened memories of your own.

Paul Winterforde-Young (centre), seen here on the Norfolk Broads, joined Butlin's in 1960 when he accepted an invitation to become Personal Advisor to Billy. Holding many posts within the company, he was responsible for heading up a project entitled 'School Venture Weeks', which Butlin's provided for schools and youth projects. This eventually became the Educational Support Service, where Paul was joined by Phil McGoldrick (left) and Diana Wall (right) and eventually this team moved the project forward until there were seventeen centres of various sizes involved.

The aim of School Venture Weeks was 'to enable and encourage children to take part in all kinds of exciting pursuits and to create a community atmosphere in which children can live and work together with people they could trust.' For children from inner cities, some of whom 'had never seen a horse without a policeman on its back or explored countryside devoid of shops and public toilets,' it was an eye-opening experience.

During the 1970s and '80s the School Venture Weeks saw up to 2,000 young people along with their teachers arriving per week to learn new skills. Children from London are seen here being aided by a member of the support staff across a stream on Exmoor during the 'Big Walk', which was held during the week at Minehead.

It is well documented that many people learnt to swim at Butlin's but here we see a group of young people at Minehead on a Cycling Proficiency course during School Venture Weeks. Volunteers from ROSPA (Royal Society for the Prevention of Accidents) taught cycling in the safe environment of the big centres and the St John Ambulance Brigade taught first aid. Certificates with national recognition were earned, and many excited and proud children left Butlin's care with knowledge and interests they would have found it hard to find back home.

This informative, fun sketch was produced by Paul Winterforde-Young to advise children and their families of the requirements to attend a School Venture Week on the Norfolk Broads. A similar list was available for each centre. How exciting it must have been to view this and know that ahead of you was a week away with the possibility of nearly forty activities of a nature previously unknown.

Opposite What an exciting prospect, walking into one of Billy's amusement parks in the late 1920s and early '30s and seeing this scene. How could anyone resist taking a ride? 'Hurrah it's Butlins!' was Billy's first slogan and over the years there have been many others. He also produced a lapel badge with these words; this was to become the first Butlin badge. Today these are greatly sought after and it is stated that a full collection could be in excess of 850 badges.

Billy always looked at a variety of options for advertising and this vehicle, seen here outside the Felixstowe Amusement Park in 1933, was just one of the early gimmicks used. He would also gain sponsorship from large organisations to sponsor events, all with an eye to promoting his company.

Cartoons have always been produced about the company, both in newspapers and magazines. During the 1970s and '80s the International Cartoonist Convention was held at Pwllheli. Before they left, the cartoonists would sign an 8ft x 4ft board with their signatures and also a small cartoon.

"They keep telling us they're going to have a new structure around here, I wonder where they're going to put it?"

Around the 1970s, the company produced a fun-filled newspaper entitled *Butlin News*, primarily for staff. It included fun features, and covered retirements, weddings, competitions, quizzes etc. Larger articles detailed who worked for many of the smaller departments, providing an intriguing glimpse into just how many staff moved around the nine centres and hotels during their employment. People generally started in basic jobs and moved around the centres to gain promotion until they led their department.

Right A 1965 entertainments programme announced the arrival of five steam locomotives 'at rest' on centres. The *Duchess of Sutherland* went to Ayr, the *Duchess of Hamilton* to Minehead, the *Royal Scot* to Skegness and the *Princess Margaret Rose* to Pwllheli. Here we see the engine arriving at Skegness, with pipes and drums announcing its arrival. Redcoats used to arrange for parties of children to view the engines up close. They were all removed from the centres between 1970 and 1974.

Below The Skegness monorail opened in 1965. It was the longest overhead rail on any camp, travelling around buildings, across the swimming pool and over chalet lines, with a station at each end. It was taken out of service in 2002 and demolished later that year.

In 1946, Billy suggested to the Archbishop of Canterbury that the Church should be available to minister to holidaymakers and staff alike. It was agreed that a resident Anglican padre be appointed at each camp and a rota of clergy was worked out. Free accommodation and meals were provided for clergymen and their families for as long as they were available from their usual parish. In addition, a Roman Catholic priest and Methodist minister from the local town would attend to provide a weekly service.

Various conferences were held, including Salvation Army, Spring Harvest, Evangelists and Assemblies of God. Staff and guests could be confirmed and in later years people have been married at the centres. Here we can see the church at Ayr in Scotland, which was just one of the purpose-built churches erected to provide a service to campers.

Billy set up the Motor Car and Motorcycle Club. He had two motorcycle patrolmen resident at each camp and every Saturday they could be seen patrolling the approach roads. Each was qualified to assist any holidaymaker who had mechanical problems. They were very distinctive in their blue uniforms on their motorbike and sidecar. During the week they carried out repairs for a moderate fee. In 1961 the cost for joining the club was 10s for a car and 5s for a motorcycle. Each member received the appropriate lapel and vehicle badge. Today these badges are very sought after. Car rallies and treasure hunts were arranged for holidaymakers with motor vehicles.

Visits to job centres were a regular occurrence during the winter months when personnel managers would travel for two or three days to major cities with a team of senior managers to advertised recruitment days. Sylvia can remember visiting the YMCA in Glasgow and finding hundreds of people queuing along the road waiting for their arrival. In addition, during the 1970s, the Mobile Job Shop (pictured), was available in certain areas to increase recruitment. During one year in Bognor Regis, the centre employed 5,000 staff, including the various short-term contracts and the main season.

The photographic department had approximately twenty seasonal staff, plus management; this consisted of a press photographer who took all official competition photographs and crowd scenes with a brief of taking 1,000 photographs weekly. A cine-operator made a film of campers during their week which they could view on Friday in the theatre. There were also five 'walkie ops', who took photographs at guests' request. Pictured here are two of the backroom staff, who were engaged in developing all films for displaying in the shop for guests to purchase.

Right On every Butlin camp you will find ladies and gentlemen's hairdressing salons, run by competent and expert staff. Butlin's Hairdressing also operated a first-class salon in London, situated in the Queensway, London W1, which was there for the convenience of all Butlin's campers, whether living in London or visiting the capital on business or holiday. Court hairdresser and managing director was Miss Mollie Rowntree, well known in London and Paris hairdressing circles, who was always on hand to help and advise.

Below Here we see Laurel and Hardy, famous comedians of the day, who in June 1947 made a personal appearance at Skegness camp and are seen here on a Social Cycle. After their appearance, they spent time with the campers and judged various competitions.

Opposite The photographic shop, shown here, obviously has an advertising arrangement with Ilford Films. Campers could hire a camera for a shilling a day, buy Ilford film and take it back to them to be developed. The bulk of their work was displaying photographs taken by the operatives in an ever-changing window display, with more boards inside. A high percentage of the photographs in this book are due to the 'walkie ops' taking shots on their daily rounds.

Patrons visiting the TOPOFTHETOWER are interested in the different floors. Here we have tried to show the layout. Kitchen at the top, Cocktail Bar and Cloakrooms, then the Revolving Restaurant. Beneath these are the Public Observation Platforms.

The Top of the Tower Restaurant was opened on 19 May 1966 by Anthony Wedgewood Benn. At 188 meters high, it was the tallest construction of the time. It was possible to obtain your Certificate of Orbit, as the restaurant turned 360 degrees. This operation was the domain of Bobbie Butlin. It was closed in 1980.

Butlin's Senior Management in 1977, on the occasion of Major Roper's retirement (he started work for the company in 1946). From left to right: Bob Webb (retail sales), Eric Carter (bookings), Bobbie Butlin (managing director), Mike Rumke (personnel controller), Frank Foulkes, Major Roper (purchasing director), Terry North (managing director, small centres) and Tony Wright (marketing director). Mr Frank Foulkes was appointed by Billy Butlin as operations director in 1965 and under his control came the expansion of the main holiday centres, the introduction of self-catering holidays and the lengthening of the season through innovative winter breaks. He was a natural leader and held in high regard by his colleagues.

From 1953, Billy was involved with the annual English Cross Channel Swim – however, his need for publicity nearly lead to his death. During the 1958 swim he donned his shorts and jumped into the water to swim the last yards with Greta Anderson, Gold Medallist, who won the £500 first prize in two consecutive years. They swam together for a time, until she went ahead and finished. Billy was left behind as the mist came down. He eventually finished and was helped out by a spectator, but did manage to have his picture taken with her.

This intriguing picture has very little information with it. This group of scuba divers are seen coming out of the sea complete with their 'Butlin's' fins and 'Butlin's' written around their waists. The only notation is that the 'Butlin team of Frogmen' made its first public appearance at the camps and thrilled campers with their amazing diving demonstrations. In the team is Gwennda Davies, believed to be the first 'frogwoman' in the world.

The immediate post-war years saw Billy using a large number of aircraft, initially painted in his colours of blue and yellow. They were also employed at Skegness, Filey and Pwllheli to provide joy rides for campers at these centres. In 1947 a flying weekend was advertised at Pwllheli where there were adequate airfield facilities at the nearby Broom Hall Estate. The number of aircraft increased until their peak in 1949. However, by the 1950s it was all over and the aircraft were sold. In the mid-1960s Butlin's again took to the air and utilised the services of television entertainer Hughie Green, who had his own aircraft and was able to help senior executives to visit sites more speedily.

Here we see Billy and Donald Campbell in 1957 along with Butlin's Head Office staff (acting as Redcoats), when they were stewards for the *Daily Mail* Paris to London Air Race. Back row, third from the left is Gus Britton. Middle row: Ron Hayter, -?-, -?-, Beryl Allen, Charlie King, -?-. Front row: Kay Kellett, -?-, -?-, Billy Butlin, Donald Campbell, Anne Hayter, -?-.

Sports personalities were always welcome at Butlin's camps and here we see Bruce Woodcock (second from the left), British and Empire heavyweight boxing champion 1945-50 and European heavyweight champion 1946-49, being served lunch. One suspects that he was supervising his meal content in the kitchens with the Butlin chefs.

The American President, Dwight D. Eisenhower, visited the UK in 1945, 1951, 1959 and 1962, staying at Culzean Castle on each occasion. During one of these visits he travelled the eight miles to see campers at the nearby Ayr holiday camp, causing quite a stir in his presidential car.

Dr Barbara Moore, who was an avid believer in healthy eating, walked from John O'Groats to Land's End; Billy thought this could be a good idea for publicity and implemented the Butlin Walk in 1960. Seven hundred and twenty-five competitors started the 1,000 mile walk and 138 finished within twenty-eight days and Billy distributed nearly £7,000 in prize money. Senior managers from the camps were brought in to act as stewards along the route. Billy flew in his own helicopter along the A6, handing glasses of champagne to the walkers.

... and finally, no matter what the weather was like, rain or sun, a holiday at Butlin's has always been an enjoyable affair. In the event of inclement weather the entertainment department put into action their 'wet weather programme.' Rain never stopped play at Butlin's.